Facing Your Feelings

Also by Bert Ghezzi

Keeping Your Kids Catholic
Becoming More Like Jesus
The Angry Christian

Facing Your Feelings

*How to Get Your Emotions
to Work for You*

Bert Ghezzi

ST. PAUL BOOKS & MEDIA

Library of Congress Cataloging-in-Publication Data

Ghezzi, Bert.
   Facing your feelings : how to get your emotions to work for you /
Bert Ghezzi.
      p. cm.
   ISBN 0-8198-2648-0
   1. Emotions—Religious aspects—Christianity. I. Title.
   BV4509.5.G463   1992
   248.4—dc20
                                                        92-16031
                                                        CIP

The Scripture quotations contained herein are from the *Revised Standard Version Bible,* Catholic Edition, copyrighted 1965 and 1966 by the
Division of Christian Education of the National Council of Churches
of Christ in the U.S.A., and are used by permision. All rights reserved.

Scripture texts indicated by an asterisk (*) are from *The Jerusalem Bible,*
copyright © 1966 by Darton, Longman & Todd, Ltd., and Doubleday
& Company, Inc. Reprinted by permission of the publisher.

ISBN 0-8198-2648-0
(previously published by Servant Books under ISBN 0-89283-133-2)

Printed and published in the U.S.A. by St. Paul Books & Media
50 St. Paul's Avenue, Boston, MA 02130.

St. Paul Books & Media is the publishing house of the Daughters of St.
Paul, an international congregation of women religious serving the
Church with the communications media.

          2 3 4 5 6 7 8   99 98 97 96 95

Contents

Introduction

How to Get the Most Out of This Book

If you're like everyone else, your emotions cause you some discomfort. Possibly, a lot of discomfort. You would like to learn how to *feel* better and you've already worked hard at it. You've probably tried a number of self-help techniques that you found in advice columns or paperbacks. You've also discovered that many of these approaches work, but that many of them don't. You may even be a little fed up with all the tidy little schemes for healing your feelings because they make you feel pressured and inadequate.

But here you go again, picking up another book that offers advice about your feelings. Even though books like this may have frustrated you in the past, I hope you read this one and use it because I think the principles it explains can be of real help to you.

I have never liked books that seem to say "if you do these five things everything will work out just fine." They always infect me with the notion that if the "five things" don't work, something is wrong with me. Now *Facing Your Feelings* is built around five principles. However, they are not presented as infallible rules, and they carry neither a warranty nor a money-back guarantee.

The five steps recommended here are simply practical things you can do to get your feelings to work for you rather than against you. When you apply these principles you can expect them to help you *feel* better. You will get more control over your emotional life, so that you can respond well to even the most powerful of feelings.

However, let me say plainly that *Facing Your Feelings* will not solve all of your emotional problems. It does not pretend to be a panacea. But it will give you a good start on your road to improved emotional health, or a boost along your way.

You will get more out of *Facing Your Feelings* if you resist trying to change a lot of things about your feelings all at once. When you attempt too much, you put yourself under pressure, which may work against you. Pressure stirs up your feelings and makes them harder for you to handle. So, don't start out trying to tackle a whole mess of problems or even one big one. It's better to begin in a small way by focusing on a little problem. Pick an area in which you think you can succeed and accumulate some successes before you take on a whopper.

Facing Your Feelings comes equipped with personal application and group discussion guides at the end of every chapter. You can skip over these pages and still benefit from the book, but I think you will get more out of it if you use them.

The book lends itself to adult religious education or study groups. A group could meet for one hour each week for six weeks. Participants would read designated sections of *Facing Your Feelings* before the group meeting. Discussion would be prompted by the questions located at the end of each chapter. The book could be divided as follows for a six-week program:

Week One	Chapters One and Two
Week Two	Chapters Three and Four
Week Three	Chapters Five and Six
Week Four	Chapter Seven
Week Five	Chapter Eight
Week Six	Chapters Nine and Ten

Facing Your Feelings is more than a self-help book. The practical Christian teaching given here shows you how to tap a power beyond yourself—the power of the Holy Spirit. You can learn how to activate God's grace in you and use it to change the ways in which you deal with your feelings. You should look for more than information about feelings or an understanding of your own emotional life in reading *Facing Your Feelings*. Read it for these reasons, but read it also as a means of spiritual growth. You should read this book prayerfully, asking the Holy Spirit to guide you, applying his wisdom to your life. That's where the real help comes from.

1

Are You What You Feel?

Not long ago, my sister, Jo Ann, called a local hospital emergency room concerning her toddler David, who had a fever of 104 degrees and was vomiting. When Jo Ann asked whether the child should be seen by a doctor, the nurse asked: "Well, how do you *feel* about it? Does his condition distress you? If it would make you feel better, you could bring him in." My sister was seeking medical advice but instead received gratuitous concern for her feelings. It happened that the child, who was seriously ill, did receive treatment.

Jo Ann was surprised that the nurse asked her how she felt rather than asking very much about the child's objective symptoms, but she should not have been. Concern for feelings is paramount in our culture. It is not an overstatement to say that our age is preoccupied with feelings. We strive to get in touch with our emotions; we catalog them, indulge them, push them down, and deny them. We care a great deal about how we feel.

In order to appreciate the extent to which our culture is dominated by concern for feelings, check out the media in your own environment.

—Analyze the content of several hours of television programming.

—Listen to the words of popular songs.

—Pay close attention to interviews on radio and television talk shows.

—Scan a dozen self-help paperbacks.

—Read the Sunday supplement and advice columns in your local paper.

—Examine several popular magazines that specialize in the personal lives of readers.

—Monitor ads and commercials.

—Read the social studies texts used in your children's schools. (One of my kids' sixth grade social studies book encouraged her to make important decisions for herself based on how she felt, rather than on what her parents said.)

With one voice, the media proclaim this message: you are what you feel.

Many Christians share this view. Secular sources have taught them the centrality of emotions, and they have learned the lesson well. People are told to begin with their feelings whenever they have a decision to make. Some pastors teach that feelings determine the course of one's life even more than goals or reasons. Keeping track of inner states and sharing about them has become for some Christians as important as prayer and Bible study.

No doubt feelings are important. They stir in us during every waking moment, filling up our consciousness with pleasant or painful promptings. Depending on their indication, they may push us toward something good or something bad. Indulging feelings can be fun or folly. To repress or ignore them is to court trouble, as we shall see in chapter four. Even so, it is a mistake to allow them to take charge of our lives. The tendency for all too many people is to over-emphasize their feelings.

Examples abound. A Protestant pastor offers other Christian leaders this advice:

Don't start with goals, start with feelings. I try to take part of Monday mornings to be alone, to get in touch with how I'm feeling about my call and my congregation.... You have to identify your feelings and then own them. I know very few ministers who can say, "I really feel jealous." ...But you have to own those feelings.[1]

Or again: a Catholic priest teaches participants in a marriage enrichment movement that the secret of learning how to love is to keep a journal, with a special focus on your feelings:

Put down the thought-feeling reactions to the outer and inner events of your life.... Feelings, in particular, are critical because they are movers. They make us go.[2]

Feelings are most emphasized in the realm of personal relationships. One popular notion of Christian love exalts emotional components like attraction and affection and downplays the elements of service and commitment. According to this view, Christian love involves understanding and reporting feelings candidly. It requires people to listen with uncritical acceptance as others share their feelings. Many popular Christian songs emphasize just such a view, with lyrics which suggest that feelings alone are the very foundation of love.

The move to put feelings first in the Christian life has been so successful that many are in danger of trading off the objective standards of the Ten Commandments and the Gospels for a life shaped only by their likes and dislikes.

More will be said about the consequences of focusing on feelings in the next chapter. It's enough for now to recognize that feelings get top billing in both secular and Christian circles.

This contemporary emphasis on emotions is a relatively new development. Were a man from, say, the thirteenth century allowed the opportunity of a brief visit to the twentieth century, he would probably be puzzled by our approach to emotions. He would be nonplussed by constant conversation about how we feel and would probably regard us as excessively introspective and moody.

Not that our visitor would be unemotional. On the contrary, he would know how to celebrate with joy, grieve over a loss, repent with remorse, and be motivated by anger or fear. He probably would be much more expressive than we are, acting out his feelings by dancing for joy, fasting in repentance, and so on.

However, he would not tend to compartmentalize his feelings as we do, relegating them to a private sphere of life and endowing them with their own inherent value. His emotions would be fully integrated into his life.

In most former societies, feelings were not isolated for special attention. Instead, emotions like anger, affection, sorrow, and fear fulfilled specific purposes within every social grouping, ranging from the family to the nation. Our friend from the thirteenth century would never have focused on a feeling, shared it with everyone he encountered, or have understood such sharing to be the essence of personal relationships. But he would have strong relationships based on loyalty, and within them he would express strong emotions.

What accounts for this difference? Why do modern people prize their emotions so? The answer lies in the changes produced by modern technological society.[3]

During the past four hundred years the constellation of material, social, political, and psychological changes called the Industrial Revolution has transformed Western society. Even a brief explanation of the complex changes brought about by industrialism would take us far afield. However, the heart of the matter is this: as a consequence of the Industrial Revolution, our society has shifted from a relational one to a functional one. In pre-industrial society everything—work, celebration, childrearing, study, emotion, and so on—was subordinated to the overarching goal of sustaining relationships and promoting the welfare of the people in those relationships. On the other hand, technological society is primarily task-oriented and, therefore, functional. Getting the job done has become all-important. The nub of the difference is that pre-industrial society valued a common life together and modern society values efficiency.

The focus on efficiency at all costs makes life seem highly impersonal. We sense that, for the most part, we are valued for what we do rather than for who we are. Many of us conclude that we are replaceable units, like workers on an assembly line. Anyone can slide a piece in place or tighten bolts. We defend ourselves from this impersonalization by separating our private from our public lives.

Because everything in the functional sphere is so impersonal, we tend to value all the more those things that seem personal. We value our feelings in particular, since they are among the more intimate elements of our personality. Confined to the personal sphere, our emotions become disconnected from outside purposes and begin to be valued primarily for their own sake. We tend, for example, to celebrate only if we *feel* happy, rather than celebrating an event of objective significance regardless of how we feel. For this reason, many people who are lonely at Christmas time sink gloomily into depression. Why should they celebrate, they ask, if they don't feel like it?

Unlike our thirteenth-century visitor, who would have expressed his feelings within the context of his relationships, we prize feelings for their own sake, rather than for how they will support our relationships. We do not make much use of our emotions to build or maintain relationships. Rather we are more interested in *feeling* our emotions. We want to savor the inner movements of joy, affection, desire, or anger. Hence our preoccupation with assuring the authenticity of our emotional life. Compartmentalizing life into the functional and personal spheres provokes some degree of emotional distress for everyone concerned. For example, anxiety, depression, guilt, insecurity, and anger are common problems in our society. We feel them deeply. We are sometimes embarrassed by them and we are concerned to do something about them.

It is one of the paradoxes of modern life that our feelings, which we are told are the source of temporal happiness, are at the same time one of our biggest problems. Feelings should neither be the cause of happiness nor of difficulty. Viewing feelings in themselves as a cause of happiness is simply an error in judgment, like trying to play a violin with a saw. Our feelings should contribute to personal strength, not erode it.

How can we get our feelings to strengthen

our character? The secret lies in caring for our emotions in the right way. The next few chapters examine two popular, but ineffective, ways to care for our feelings. Remaining chapters present a strategy based on Scripture and Christian experience, which works to engage our feelings in support of Christian behavior.

For Personal Reflection and Application

Take stock of the role one feeling plays in your life.

1. Select one of the following feelings: anger, aversion, fear, grief, guilt, joy, self-esteem, or sexual desire.

2. Use these questions to assess how you experience that feeling:

How often do I experience this feeling? _____

_____

What does it feel like? _____

_____

Do I enjoy it? _____

Do I do anything to stir it up? If so, what?

_____

_____

What do I usually do in response to it?

_____

_____

_____

_____

Does it cause me any problems? If so, describe them. _____

_____

_____

_____

Do I sometimes wish the feeling would go away? _____

Have I talked about it with another person?

_____

Do I seek help with it? _____

Have I ever read a book or article about it?

_____

Have I ever prayed about it? _____

For Discussion

1. Is the statement "You are what you feel" an accurate observation? Why or why not?

2. In your opinion, how extensive is concern for feelings in our culture?

3. How do we handle emotions differently from people in earlier societies?

4. What factors influence contemporary people to pay so much attention to their feelings?

2

Focusing on Feelings

Most people want their feelings to contribute positively to their lives. Consequently, they look for ways to make their emotions work better. At hand are numerous contemporary techniques for dealing with emotional problems. Most of these techniques are rooted in the humanistic self-psychology of Eric Fromm, Carl Rogers, and others. These theorists teach that the self reaches its true potential by making choices based primarily on feelings.[4]

Therapists, encounter groups, creativity workshops, and university classrooms have popularized the ideas of these men. A myriad of self-help paperbacks, many of them reaching millions, continue to persuade people that the way to care for their feelings is to follow after them. Popularizers of selfish theories assert the primacy of feelings over every other faculty: "My perception of my reality and the choice I make which follows must be based on what I feel. This is not surprising, inasmuch as my feelings tend to represent all aspects of myself relatively free of diluting outside influences.... While I prefer to trust and to tap my integrated feeling and intellectual self, if they are at odds, I have learned that I do better in my behalf to listen to the music rather than the words. The music represents how I feel."[5]

Or listen to the advice that follows. It may seem extreme, but the advice that this doctor offers captures the popular mind about putting feelings in charge: "The world is a puzzle each of us assembles differently. But each of us can learn to deal with it by using our natural gifts in a more effective way—which includes learning to feel more honestly. The more honest you become the more energy you will have to deal with the problems you face.... If you don't live in your feelings, you don't live in the real world. Feelings are the truth."[6]

Millions of ordinary people have bought into this thinking and are attempting to make the most of their feelings by giving them free rein.

The Driftwood Approach

Modern techniques for helping us fine tune our feelings are sometimes couched in sophisticated terms. But beneath the sophistication lies a fairly simple assumption: our feelings are facts of life. Like principles of mathematics, they cannot be changed. The best way to deal with them, we are told, is to follow them wherever they lead. Consider this observation on the power of moods:

> I see moods as complex combinations of feelings and I see all moods as human and acceptable, even murderous moods. We are, remember, speaking of moods, not actions. We must permit and accept such varied moods as feeling lazy, full of vitality, happy, sad, sexy, repulsive, seclusive, charming, cold, luxurious, stingy, vulnerable, tough, fragile, irritable, abrasive, sensitive, nostalgic, lonely, ungiving, sentimental, beautiful, ugly, masterful, childish, loving, old, wise, dumb and many others, including great mixtures of all these moods, which are for the most part indescribable in mere words.... Moods seldom remain static for long. They keep changing as they respond to the vast admixture of feelings emanating from our own psyches and affected by stimuli

from outside ourselves. Sometimes we can control or even change a mood, but this is relatively rare.[7]

This approach views emotions as vital energies that pass through us. They move with great strength, alternating from one feeling to another and flowing like a fast-moving stream. We could stand against the onrush of emotions, but that would only cause us pain. Rivers gradually erode rocks that oppose them. Feelings that are denied wear us down far more quickly—so the teaching goes. Better to be like driftwood, flowing with our feelings. At one time I feel happy; then I feel bored; next I feel hurt; later I feel angry. I move from one emotional state to another, or more accurately, my emotional states move me along from one moment to another.

The driftwood approach encourages people to welcome every feeling that comes no matter how repugnant it may seem. This view holds that negative attitudes toward certain emotions are culturally conditioned: "Our culture views certain feelings and moods as pejorative and even abhorrent and antithetical to the state of being human. I have seen so many people who say, 'I don't know what is the matter with me. I feel so lazy' or 'so vulnerable' or 'so touchy' or so 'dopy and childish' or 'so lonely,' and on and on it goes. This is largely a function of cultural prejudice. Moods should require no justification whatsoever. As with little children who feel the way they feel simply *because*, we, too, must be permitted to feel because we feel."[8]

The driftwood approach has become very popular. And on occasion it can even be helpful, as when used to awaken people to their internal states as an aid in resolving emotional problems. But adopting the driftwood approach as the normal way of handling feelings is tantamount to putting them in charge.

Focus on Feelings

Another popular approach to handling emotions is to focus on feelings. The goal here is to communicate how you feel with complete honesty. You reflect on your experience of the feeling and attempt to describe it as graphically as possible. This technique has been popularized in both secular and Christian encounter-group movements.

It is illustrated through sharings like the one that follows from an Australian Christian marriage-enrichment bulletin. Under the title "How to focus on feelings and not to drift off into being judgmental," two letters from Harry to Mavis are contrasted. In the first, Harry explains how angry he feels because he has woken up six times during the previous night to attend to a sick child. Throughout the night, Mavis "didn't move even once." Mavis responds: "I'm sorry, Harry, but I can't seem to get any feelings at all about your letter." So to help his wife appreciate his feelings and to avoid what is criticized as "garbage dumping" in his first letter, Harry wrote the following, a classic example of the focus-on-feelings genre:

My dearest,

The best way to describe the feelings I have now, about last night, is cold and distant. It's a really rotten feeling, Mavis, and I almost wish I didn't have to describe how I feel to you. I feel cut off from you—an aloof, don't-touch-me sort of feeling—and one which also makes me want to avoid touching you. I feel all prickly, like I'm surrounded by blackberry bushes, or like a snail which goes into its shell as soon as you touch it.

Mavis, I feel so really cold and horrible inside. It's almost as if I'm wearing a mask, friendly enough—or polite—but distant. Like one of those butlers you see in an old movie. My face and body feel stiff, set in a mold and I really find it hard to smile.... It's almost as if I were in an old cellar, water dripping down the walls, no windows and a single, dirty globe hanging from the ceiling. Everything is so gray, hopeless and I feel so alone and cut off from everyone. Especially from you, my darling.[9]

The commentator observed that this letter "laid the foundation for a deeper sharing of feelings." According to him, it offered an opportunity "for their relationship to grow stronger." This kind of sharing about feelings elevates emotions, placing them above such fundamental values as forgiveness and common decency.

In some Christian circles the focus-on-feeling approach is associated with prayer for inner healing. Advocates of this method encourage Christians to spend time each day seeking healing for their hurts. The practice normally involves honestly and prayerfully describing to Christ one's feelings about those who have injured one. When this is done, the person is encouraged to stir up feelings of forgiveness toward the guilty parties. In fact, praying with others about an emotional problem can bring new freedom in an area that was previously locked up. But daily reviewing hurt feelings is not very helpful because a constant focus-on-feelings puts them in control.

People who focus on their feelings often

keep a journal. They record their inward journey, describing their feelings in detail in an attempt to understand themselves better.

Psychotherapists have developed a technique which requires patients to keep track of their emotional states. As a clinical technique for curing people with serious emotional problems, this practice has great value. But as a tool for daily personal life, keeping a journal of our feelings may weaken rather than strengthen us. Taking stock of our self and our inward state can be a source of strength if it points to areas where growth or change is needed. However, focusing on our feelings daily and writing about them extensively puts emotions in charge in a way that can cause problems. Making feelings the master of our lives requires more of them than they were designed to deliver.

For Personal Reflection and Application

1. What feelings do I experience most strongly?

_____

_____

2. What do I do when I experience these feelings? _____

_____

_____

_____

For Discussion

1. Which do you think is the most important: your intellect, your will, or your feelings? Why?

2. What is "the driftwood approach" to feelings? What is the understanding of emotions behind this approach?

3. What is "the focus-on-feelings" approach to handling emotions?

3

Do Feelings
Run Your Life?

A technique for handling our emotions will appeal to us if it works. We expect it to help us attain a healthy emotional life by freeing us from disorders. As Christians we want the approach we adopt to help us to serve God more effectively and to enable us to become more like Christ. So we must test strategies for dealing with feelings to determine whether they are *effective* and whether they *conform to Christian principles.*

Both the driftwood and the focus-on-feelings approaches are guided by the belief that emotions are our masters and must be allowed to direct the course of our lives. We might resist this evaluation so baldly stated, but a little reflection should persuade us of its validity. As we have seen, neither secular nor Christian advocates of these strategies hide their conviction that feelings should govern us:

"Don't start with goals, start with feelings."

"Feelings...are critical because they are the movers."

"If you don't live in your feelings, you don't live in the real world. Feelings are the truth."

"As with little children who feel the way they feel simply *because*, we, too, must be permitted to feel because we feel."

Common sense tells us that something is wrong with the notion that emotions should run our lives. Our experience with fear, desire, guilt feelings, and anger should be enough to persuade us that our emotions do not always guide us well. Whatever they are to be for us, they should not be our masters. This is not to deny their value, for even those that we sometimes mistakenly view as destructive, like fear and anger, can be good and useful.

The flaws of the feelings-as-master strategies stand out in sharp relief when the tests of effectiveness and conformity to Christian teaching are applied. Putting feelings in charge does not work well as a method for resolving emotional problems. In fact, this approach can generate new problems. Besides being ineffective, the feelings-as-master approach results in unchristian attitudes and behavior.

When we experience an emotional reaction, we need first and foremost a way to express it. If we are grief-stricken because a relative has died, it will help to view the body, to weep and throw dirt on the coffin as it is lowered into the grave. If we are angry about something, we may be moved to act, perhaps to speak forcefully to a co-worker or to change a difficult situation. If we experience fear, it may motivate us to meet a particular danger head-on or to run, whichever seems most prudent. But in the midst of an emotional reaction, usually the last thing we need to do is to encourage ourselves to greater intensity of feeling.

Yet intensification of feeling is the very thing that the focus-on-feeling approach aims at. According to practitioners of this approach, the goal is to experience the raw energy of the emotion as fully as possible. This solution may create worse problems than those we started with. Instead of bringing relief, it increases our discomfort.

The effect is worse when we apply the technique to emotional problems that last for a period of time. Feeling bad about oneself, for example, is a common emotional difficulty. If a person with this problem adopts the focus-on-feeling approach, the problem will only worsen. Exploring the inner reaches of these feelings will only give such a person more reason for self-hatred. The remedy comes from focusing on goals outside oneself, such as serving other people, rather than focusing on feeling inadequate, incompetent, or hateful.

Unruly sexual desire is another case in point. Sexual desire in itself is good since it motivates us to cooperate in God's plan to establish new families through the union of husband and wife. However, persistent sexual desires can dominate the attention of both married and single people until they develop sizeable emotional problems. Paying more attention to such desires only increases their power. Any fourteen-year-old boy can tell you that if you focus on a sexual feeling it will become more intense. If a person is taking the driftwood approach, who knows where unruly sexual desires will lead?

Neither will a guilt-ridden person find help in focusing on guilt feelings. If anything, the more people perceive their guilt in detail the more guilty they will feel. The very process of exploring guilt feelings magnifies their conviction of guilt. They need to do something other than probe their feelings; they must deal responsibly with the guilt.

This analysis holds true when applied to other feelings, such as anxiety, irritability, and insecurity. The feelings-in-charge models don't work, and can even increase a person's emotional difficulties.

Moodiness and Passivity

Introspection is a tool commonly employed in the feelings-as-master approaches. A glance inward now and then can be helpful, but continuous introspective staring rarely helps. People who are preoccupied with their feelings turn in on themselves and may be perceived by others as withdrawn. Habitual introspection makes them subject to their moods. Drifting from one mood to the next does not confer emotional freedom on a person. It just makes for moodiness.

Some claim, as we have seen, that moods need no justification. Maybe so, but that does not make them any less difficult for us. A rock needs no justification, but when it blocks my path it's an obstacle. Verbal gymnastics cannot flip the truth: moodiness is an emotional problem. The prescription for its cure is the opposite of focus-on-feelings. Moody people must cease turning inward and begin to reach outward to serve others.

Excessive inwardness also leads to passivity and unhealthy preoccupation with self. People may even become so caught up in "exploring their interior space" that they are unable to function in normal daily life:

> Each of us with fabulous clarity can proclaim, "There's a child born with my name and my destiny...! I can choose to peek inward. I can allow myself to be jolted, to experience the fright that comes to one who is being reborn!"

> I remember feeling the emptiness, the darkness, the separateness, the cruel and savage power of transformative fright.... I felt paralyzed and unable to be objective. It took so much energy to attend to the interior demands that I could not believe that I was functioning at all as the father, the husband, the working person I wanted to be. I groped and surrendered my way one long inch at a time.[10]

The man in this extreme example described his inward journey into a terrible loneliness and savage fear that "paralyzed" him. For three years his preoccupation with his emotional states consumed so much energy that he doubted whether he was able to perform his duties as husband and father.

Emotion-dominated persons may offend by omission. This approach to feelings drains them of the strength to do the things they are supposed to do. Focus-on-feelings makes us passive because it sidetracks us from important action.

Unchristian Attitudes and Behavior

Selfishness and wrongdoing are the most serious dangers in the emotions-as-master mentality. Christianity is thoroughly other-directed. Jesus taught us to live singleheartedly for God and to love others by laying down our life for them. If we want to gain our life, we must lose ourselves—this is at the core of his message. The feelings-in-charge approach leads in the opposite direction. Not only do we become so absorbed by our feelings that we have no time for others; we also become possessed by self-concern as a consequence of constantly turning inward to care for our feelings.

This self-indulgence prevents us from relating to others Christianly. Christian parents may go adrift in their feelings and fail to care for their family. Christians may be hurt by others' gossip. They nurse their hurt feelings, try to stir up feelings of forgiveness, but stop short of the biblical command to forgive offenders.

Some Christians who advocate the emotions-as-master approach have elevated feelings to such heights that they place concern for them above Christian standards of behavior.

> I hope my wife will never divorce me, because I love her with all my heart. But if one day she feels that I am minimizing her or making her feel inferior or in any way standing in the light that she needs to become the person that God meant her to be, I hope she'll be free to throw me out even if she's one hundred. There is something more important than our staying married, and it has to do with integrity, personhood, and purpose.[11]

It also seems to have something to do with a self-indulgent approach to emotions. Lifelong openness to growth is a good thing. There are limits, however, and subordinating the Christian teaching on divorce to feelings goes beyond them.

Theories such as the one stated in the previous quote have practical ramifications. Who doesn't know at least one couple who got in touch with their feelings one year and got divorced the next? Christians are not immune from such consequences, and neither are Christian leaders who teach that feelings should control one's life.

In 1970 Robert Raines attended a training group seminar that changed his life. In a recent book, *Going Home*, Raines, who is now the director of Kirkridge Retreat Center in Bangor, Pennsylvania, describes the T-group, which was sponsored by the National Training Laboratories of Bethel, Maine.

The T-group brought together fourteen people who probed and commented on one another's personalities for two weeks. The principal effect on him, Raines reports, was that the seminar stirred up some very strong feelings. "I got in touch with anger that I had stored up for decades," he writes. He discovered that he was angry at God, the Church, his father, himself, and his wife, Peggy.

"When I returned from the Bethel experience," Raines writes, "Peggy and I had our frankest talk ever." The two decided that Peggy should also attend a T-group. "There she got in touch with her own anger...she returned with those feelings churned up and raw.

"And for the next several years we both worked on our own angry feelings. It was a lot to work on individually, much less to be doing it at the same time. It was the beginning of the end for us as a couple, an end that although wrenching and sad proved to be a healthy new beginning for each of us in our own way."[12]

Emotions that are allowed to rule can push us to wrongdoing. Grief can become a hideous self-pity that poisons relationships. Anger-in-control (which, according to Scripture, is always sinful) can drive us to fights, broken relationships, even murder. Sexual attraction (disguised as "romance") can lead to fornication or marital infidelity (disguised as "developing mature relationships") and so on. It's easy to see where the road leads if we decide to follow our feelings.

For Personal Reflection and Application

1. Is any one feeling dominant in my life? Which one? _____

2. Has this feeling ever helped me? How?

_____

3. Has this feeling ever hurt me or got me in trouble? How? _____

_____

_____

4. Do I tend to regard some of my feelings as "masters"? Which ones? _____

_____

5. Why do I take that approach to these feelings?

_____

_____

_____

For Discussion

1. Why must we test strategies for handling our feelings?

2. Why is putting feelings in charge an ineffective way of dealing with our emotions?

3. What is the danger of constant introspection?

4. How do "feelings-as-master" approaches lead to self-indulgence?

5. In what ways can putting feelings in charge lead to unchristian behavior?

4

Are You Afraid
of Your Feelings?

By now you may think that just about every-body gives free rein to their emotions. If so, perhaps I should apologize for misleading you. Nero Wolfe, Rex Stout's fat, eccentric detective genius, says he favors the Anglo-Saxon approach to emotions and dessert: "freeze them and hide them in your belly." Many people agree wholeheartedly with Wolfe. As a result, they take a very defensive approach to their feelings. You will even find some people who mix their approaches. For instance, they may vent their anger furiously at the same time that they suppress their sexual desires. Or vice versa.

Most people find a certain set of emotions to be troublesome. The list includes anger, anxiety, depression, guilt, insecurity, self-hatred, grief, fear, and unruly desire, to name the prominent ones. Sometimes people form the mistaken opinion that these emotions are always destructive and must be avoided at all costs. Certainly, some of these are always harmful: can you think of constructive self-hatred? But most of the list—anger, fear, and desire, to be sure—should bring us more good than harm. That they damage us is frequently due to the way we approach them.

We tend to relate to bothersome emotions as though they are our enemies. Fear is usually what motivates defensive behavior. Our anger can easily escalate into uncontrollable rage; ugly past behavior makes us fearful of possible violent reactions in the future. Anxiety may have immobilized us before and the hint of a repeat performance intimidates us.

Other factors, too, may cause us to battle our emotions. Bouts with guilt feelings can make us so uncomfortable that we feel compelled to quash them. Shame may lead us to resist sexual desires because we do not want anyone, including ourselves, to find out that we have them. We may have to look for a way to conceal our desire for revenge from ourselves because vengeance does not fit the image of the kind and loving person we want to be.

Desire to protect ourselves from having to change is yet another motive for denying our feelings. We may swallow our anger at a subordinate's laziness because we don't want to deal with his reaction when he's corrected. Or perhaps we protect ourselves from guilt feelings because we don't want to stop behaving wrongly.

To combat these feelings, we arm ourselves with mechanisms that enable us to avoid, deny, or freeze them within. Tactics for insulating us from our feelings may work either unconsciously or deliberately. *Repression* is a technical term for unconsciously ignoring or denying a feeling that annoys us. For example, a boy may repress feelings of hostility toward his father. These feelings are inconsistent with his notion of what it means to be a good son. He does not repress the emotion deliberately; he merely behaves toward his father as though the hostile feeling did not exist.

Suppression is another very common defense mechanism. When we suppress a feeling we deliberately push it down. Guilt feelings may nag a person who has been stealing from his employer. He may have to aggressively suppress those feelings in order to proceed with his thievery. A student who anticipates imminent failure may decide to suppress his anxiety because he cannot bring himself to consider what life would be like without a college degree.

When it comes to protecting ourselves from feelings we do not like, we can invent a number of creative maneuvers to avoid them. Sometimes we deny a bothersome feeling by engaging in behavior that expresses the exact opposite feeling. A person who is plagued by feelings of inferiority might insulate himself from them by acting extremely superior. A youth might dissociate himself from his sexual feelings by pretending to himself and others that he hates girls. He may try to prove this by treating them despicably.

We may attempt to rid ourselves of an undesirable emotion by directing it against someone or something. If a man is angry because his boss criticizes him publicly, he may express it by exploding at his wife (and she at the children, and they at the pets). Whether we employ these tactics deliberately or unconsciously, they are designed to deal with feelings that we regard as enemies.

The Stern Disciplinarian

In addition to these tactics for handling "enemy" emotions, we often take a more direct approach. We can decide to subdue the emotions by the exercise of strict discipline, thus hoping to eliminate the distress they cause us. I call this the stern disciplinarian approach, in honor of all school teachers who have tried by sheer personal force to bring order out of chaos in a classroom of animated, but disobedient children. The stern disciplinarian, by constant vigilance and rigid enforcement of rules, might bring superficial peace to the classroom. But let her drop her guard for a moment and watch the confusion erupt.

People who decide to take the stern disciplinarian approach to their emotions are usually motivated by a sincere desire for improvement. Consider the man who observes that anger is making a shambles of his life. He decides he will allow himself no more outbursts. He determines to use every ounce of willpower to keep the lid on his anger. You have seen this fellow, haven't you? He's the red-faced man, seething with rage through gritted teeth, who thinks he is controlling his temper.

A modest exercise of willpower may help, as we shall see in later chapters. But the attempt to control emotions by sheer willpower is mistaken and ineffective.

None of the approaches described in this chapter pass the pragmatic test for caring for our feelings. They simply do not work. Much like aspirin for a headache, they bring only temporary relief at best. None of these remedies are able to tap the good in these feelings, channelling them into some constructive behavior. Such feelings, defined as harmful, remain liabilities, to be avoided or defeated whatever the cost.

Consider the lad who represses hostile feelings towards his father. Repression may prevent him from experiencing the feeling, but it has not diffused the hostility. Hostility is alive and well beneath the surface. Sooner or later it will express itself in the boy's behavior. The father will attempt to be friendly, and the boy will respond with cold silence; the boy will do poorly in school simply because his father hopes he will learn well. Whatever it takes to cure the hostility, clearly, repression or any of the feelings-as-enemy approaches will never do it. The same is true for suppressed guilt feelings, submerged anxiety, the stern disciplinarian approach, and so on. We can pretend that hiding a time-bomb in the closet will protect the house from danger, but eventually it will blow the building to pieces.

Abused emotions tend to multiply our problems, sometimes very seriously. Repressed anger can plunge us into chronic depression, and repressed sexual feelings can result in psychosexual illnesses. Freezing and hiding strong feelings within us can make us physically ill.

The more advanced emotional problems triggered by emotions-as-enemy tactics are hard to cure, as any Christian pastor or competent psychological counselor will tell you. Emotions treated like enemies will behave like enemies and retaliate.

We have seen that treating emotions as masters is risky because giving our feelings free rein can lead us to sin. The same is true of approaching our emotions as enemies. Defense mechanisms merely hide the problem; they don't correct it nor do they bring good out of the strong feelings which they attempt to control. If we simply push down our emotions, they will wait, determined to collect their due. When they finally emerge, they may move us to wrongdoing.

Of course, a person may have sufficient strength of character to resist sinning, but suppressed emotion has the power to motivate even the strong to unrighteous acts. For example, if a person consistently suppresses sexual desires and takes no other steps to handle these strong feelings, such desires will continue to exert pressure from their hiding place. A person may have the fortitude to behave righteously, but not without great struggle. Suppressed sexual feelings have been known to win contests over the clearest intellect and the strongest will. Such a person may repeat over and over "I'm not going to give in" all along the way to a rendezvous with adultery.

We are also familiar with the dangerous potential of bottled up anger. If it comes out—and it normally finds a way—it will probably move us to behave sinfully. When anger takes control we regularly harm others by violent speech or violent deeds. Even anger that is "safely" tucked away can cause us to behave unrighteously. Tricks sponsored by suppressed anger include the cold shoulder, the snub, and withholding affection. These can do as much violence to relationships as slander or an outright fight.

Stoicism

Christians have sometimes made the mistake of thinking that suppression constitutes a Christian approach to dealing with emotions. Extreme versions hold that the feelings themselves are wicked and to be avoided at all costs. Sexual desire and anger are two emotions, for example, that some Christians regard as always sinful, to be dealt with as enemies. Christians who believe the emotions are intrinsically evil may try to be completely unaffected by their feelings.

People who take this approach become more stoic than Christian. Stoicism was an ancient Greek philosophical movement which taught that the source of unhappiness is our emotional reaction to things beyond our personal control. The only way to happiness for the stoic was the methodical control of feelings, painstakingly training them not to react to external stimuli. Stoicism had many wise things to say about human nature, much of it valuable today, but its core principle was off the mark. Frustration, not happiness, results from habitual denial of emotional reactions.

We have now questioned the two most popular approaches to dealing with emotions. Both the feelings-as-master and the feelings-as-enemy approaches are ineffective and unchristian. A less popular, but more effective way to deal with emotions does exist. It is an approach that transforms our emotions into strengths. This biblically based way of facing our feelings is the subject of the remaining chapters.

For Personal Reflection and Application

1. What feelings do I find the most troublesome?

_____

2. Which emotion or emotions do I feel are always my downfall? _____

_____

3. How do I react to the following feelings? (Decide which reaction most accurately describes your response to each feeling.)

Common reactions:

Ignore it.   Fear it.
Give it free rein.   Enjoy it.
Push it down.   Do something about it.
Indulge it.   Change my behavior.
Pretend it's not there.

Troublesome Feelings:	*How I react:*
Anger	_____
Anxiety	_____
Depression	_____
Fear	_____
Hatred	_____
Insecurity	_____

Jealousy	_____
Loneliness	_____
Low self-esteem	_____
Selfishness	_____
Sexual desire	_____
Worry	_____

4. Which of these difficult feelings have the potential to become positive factors for me?

_____

For Discussion

1. Why do some of our feelings cause us trouble?

2. Describe some ways in which we try to defend ourselves from bad feelings.

3. What does it mean to repress an emotion? Give an example of repression.

4. What does it mean to suppress a feeling? Give an example of suppression.

5. What is the "stern disciplinarian" approach?

6. How well do these defense mechanisms work in handling our feelings? Why?

7. Are emotions ever bad in themselves?

8. What is the Christian objection to the stoic approach to feelings?

5

Feelings as Assets

Many people tend to think of their feelings as liabilities. If they had the option, they would probably choose to have their emotions surgically removed, much like inflamed tonsils or a ruptured appendix. This view of emotions-as-nuisance attracts us to the stratagems previously criticized. As other things about us, like our body or our will, our feelings are potential liabilities. Dealing with them simply as nuisances guarantees that they will fulfill their potential.

If we discard popular approaches to handling our emotions, what is left to us? Are we stuck with our problems, forced to endure them day in and day out until we die? No, we have an alternative, a Christian approach to caring for emotions, based on Scripture and proven to be successful in thousands of people's lives.

Feelings Are Basically Good

The Christian approach begins with the truth that our feelings are good. God has designed them for our benefit and made them standard equipment in every human being. A truly unemotional person does not exist. Anyone who appears to be without feelings is either repressing them or is unbalanced in some way and in need of help.

God made emotions good and assigned them each a purpose. Emotions used in accord with God's intention are not liabilities, but resources for our lives. The word "emotion" is derived from a Latin word (*emovere*) which literally means "to move out," "to stir up," and "to agitate." Our experience of feelings testifies to the accuracy of this name. Emotions work by agitating us. They stir in us, and we can stir them up. Emotions move us out, incite us, drive us, and urge us. They prompt us in some direction. Motivation, a word based on the same Latin root, accurately expresses the purpose of emotions. In collaboration with our intellect and will, emotions are supposed to motivate us to action.

The following brief list, which defines certain emotions in terms of their purposes, illustrates the point.

Anger is a strong agitation impelling us to deal with an unacceptable situation, perhaps opposition, injury, or mistreatment. Anger is a God-given tool for breaking through obstacles. Therefore, it is very useful for getting us through a day, let alone a lifetime.

Joy refers to delight which leads us to celebrate events such as an act of God (healing us, blessing us with prosperity) or personal landmarks (births, weddings). As an emotional state, joy sparks us to express our gladness, perhaps by singing, dancing, or feasting.

Fear means being in awe of someone or something greater and more powerful than oneself. The purpose of fear is to motivate us to behave correctly in the presence of one greater than we are, for example, before God. Fear is at the core of the disposition we call respect. It motivates us to relate well to people we should honor, such as parents, spouses, leaders, and so on. Care and concern are forms of fear that can motivate us to handle our responsibilities thoroughly and faithfully. Another kind of fear serves as an inner warning, signaling us to be ready to act courageously in the face of danger.

Desire is intended to draw us toward something that is good for us. For example, desire attracts a mother to her baby, to motivate her to care for it well. Or desire draws young people to ideals beyond themselves, motivating them to live generously for others.

Aversion is the opposite of desire and its purpose is to repel us from anything evil or inimical to us such as sin or the devil. A healthy aversion to witchcraft, false religion, sexual perversion, and so on has always been a protection for Christians.

Grief motivates us to express our sorrow over some loss, disaster, or misfortune. God intended us to recognize the pain that death causes and to bring it to resolution through appropriate customs expressing our grief. Thus, grief helps us accept our loss, adjust to it, and move ahead in our lives, serving the Lord and others.

Our feelings are basically good when used in accord with their purpose. As such they are valuable assets for our daily life. If we have rarely experienced our feelings as anything other than liabilities, then our emotions are not working as they were intended. The Christian view holds that they are the Creator's gifts, not mistakes, and that they should be advantages, not obstacles.

Feelings in Scripture

Since Scripture does not discuss feelings at length, we cannot turn to a particular section for a summary. But the Bible teaches throughout that feelings are good and valuable. Consider, for example, the various scriptural commands involving some emotional response:

"Fear him who, after he has killed, has power to cast into hell" (Lk 12:5).

"Fear God" (1 Pt 2:17).

"Be angry but do not sin" (Eph 4:26).

"Rejoice always" (1 Thes 5:16).

"Love one another with brotherly affection" (Rom 12:10a).

"Weep with those who weep" (Rom 12:15).

Paul refers to these terse directions as "army orders" (1 Thes 4:2). They were typical of the practical teaching regarded as essential by early Christian pastors. Clearly, Scripture commands us to engage in Christian conduct which involves expressing strong feelings. The New Testament seems to put a priority on these commands, indicating that emotions are good and integral to effective Christian living.

While Scripture does not offer a treatise on the emotions, it does present excellent examples of the way feelings should work in our lives. The people we meet in the Bible used their emotions instinctively as a normal part of living. If we look at those held up for our imitation—the Apostle Paul and Jesus himself—we see that they expressed their emotions as part of the correct human response to the situations in which they found themselves.

Paul served others out of *agape*, the love of commitment. But, as his letters show, he was also motivated by strong personal affection and a desire to be with those he had recruited into the kingdom. He writes from prison to the Christians at Philippi, expressing a deep, almost tangible desire to be with them: "For God is my witness, how I yearn for you all with the affection of Christ Jesus" (Phil 1:8). When jail keeps him from those he loves, Paul longs for them in a deeply human way. We can see him react the same way in his letter to the Thessalonians. "A short time after we had been separated from you—in body but never in thought, brothers—we had an especially strong desire and longing to see you face to face again, and we tried hard to come and visit you" (1 Thes 2:17).*

Desire moved strongly in Jesus too. "I have earnestly desired to eat this passover with you before I suffer" (Lk 22:15), he told his apostles at the Last Supper. As the Lord anticipated imminent death, his yearning to celebrate this last Passover supper with his most intimate co-workers and friends is understandable to all of us. It was a healthy human emotional reaction.

The most interesting biblical example of emotion as the correct response to a situation occurs in the account of the resurrection of Lazarus. John makes it plain that the Lord knew from the outset that he would call Lazarus back from death to life. Yet Jesus was overcome with grief when he saw the tomb that held his dead friend. The Gospel writer says, "Jesus wept." When he approached the cave, Jesus was "deeply moved again" (Jn 11:35, 38). It seems to make no sense for him to weep for a man he knew he was going to raise from the dead. But Jesus loved Lazarus with great affection. Grief was the natural emotional response to Lazarus' death, and Jesus expressed his grief instinctively.

In fact, Jesus manifested the whole range of human emotions. The seventy disciples returned from preaching the Gospel with power, and Jesus, delighted in their accomplishments, "rejoiced in the Holy Spirit" (Lk 10:21). Compassion impelled him to heal the sick: "Moved with pity, he stretched out his hand and touched him, and said to him, 'I will; be clean.' And immediately the leprosy left him" (Mk 1:41-42). He was angered and grieved by the opposition of the Pharisees to his mission (cf. Mk 3:5). In the face of death, he went to Gethsemane, where he "began to be greatly distressed and troubled," and he said to the three apostles he had taken along, "My soul is very sorrowful, even to death" (Mk 14:33, 34). When feelings were appropriate, Jesus expressed them in normal human ways.

The scriptural teaching on feelings emerges clearly from the example of Jesus and Paul. Emotions are to be supportive elements in our lives, a part of the right human response to everyday events. In sum, Scripture assumes that our feelings are supposed to help us do things right.

The Bible teaches further that feelings should help us in our Christian service. Our emotions can strengthen us by motivating us to accomplish our work for the Lord more effectively. Look again at the example of Jesus and Paul, whose emotional reactions helped them do the will of God.

We are all familiar with the account of Jesus' indignation at the money-changers in the Temple. Anger stirred in the Lord because of the desecration of his Father's dwelling, and he engaged his wrath to expel the offenders. Anger motivated Paul to take authority over the evil spirit that hounded him through the slave girl at Philippi, resulting in the girl's freedom and ultimately in the conversion of the local jailer and his entire household (cf. Acts 16:16ff.).

Indignation and desire impelled Paul to preach the Good News. Luke says that while Paul was in Athens, "his spirit was provoked within him as he saw that the city was full of idols" (Acts 17:16). This anger moved Paul to present the Gospel, debating with the Athenian Jews and discussing the Good News openly in the marketplace.

Paul recalls that his fondness for the Thessalonians made him eagerly desire their conversion. "But we were gentle among you, like a nurse taking care of her children. So, being affectionately desirous of you, we were ready to share with you not only the gospel of God but also our own selves, because you had become very dear to us" (1 Thes 2:7-8). Paul trusted that his desires would help him accomplish his mission, and he followed his inclinations whenever they advanced the Gospel.

Scripture also shows how grief, fear and joy can move us to obey God. When Ezra learned that the returned exiles had defied God and intermarried with their pagan neighbors, he was grief stricken. He rent his garments, wailed, cast himself on the ground, and fasted. His grief inspired sorrow in the hearts of others, so that they corrected their wrongdoing by separating themselves from their foreign wives and children (cf. Ezr 9, 10). Ezra's expression of strong emotion helped him correct a seriously sinful condition. Similarly, grief supported the Corinthians in their repentant response to Paul's forceful corrections: "See what earnestness this godly grief has produced in you, what eagerness to clear yourselves, what indignation, what alarm, what longing, what zeal, what punishment!" (2 Cor 7:11)

Preaching the Gospel to Jews and pagans in the Roman Empire was a risky business. The message captivated people and seemed to disrupt the accepted order of things. This danger awakened fear in Paul (cf. 2 Cor 7:5), but instead of immobilizing him, it egged him on to greater boldness. The other apostles certainly knew fear as they began to witness to some of the very people who had clamored for Jesus' crucifixion. They seized upon fear as an opportunity for courageous proclamation of the Good News.

Christian service brings with it the promise of suffering, as Paul well knew. But when he was afflicted from all sides—"fighting without and fear within"—joy strengthened him for endurance (2 Cor 7:5, 7). Joy strengthened the Lord himself at the climax of his mission: "Let us run with perseverance the race that is set before us, looking to Jesus the pioneer and perfecter of our faith, who for the joy that was set before him endured the cross, despising the shame, and is seated at the right hand of the throne of God" (Heb 12:1-2). The joy of eternal happiness is a spiritual quality, but since it is a gift for human beings, it also has an emotional component so that we can anticipate the joy that will be ours in eternity.

The Christian approach to feelings gives them a higher place and a more significant role than our experience with them might at first seem to warrant. But Scripture is clear on the subject. Emotions are valuable assets, resources to assist us in faithfully serving God.

Now comes the problem. This may very well be the teaching of Scripture about feelings, but what if our experience demonstrates that emotions have not helped us very much in our Christian lives?

For Personal Reflection and Application

For each of the feelings in the following list:
1. State how the feeling can be helpful.
2. Give an example of how that has helped you in the past.

Anger
1. _____
2. _____
_____
_____

Joy
1. _____
2. _____
_____
_____

Fear
1. _____
2. _____
_____
_____

Desire
1. _____

2._____

_____

_____

Aversion

1._____

2._____

_____

_____

Grief

1._____

2._____

_____

_____

For Discussion

1. Why can it be said that feelings are basically good?

2. What purpose do emotions have in our lives. Give examples, if possible from your experience.

3. What does Scripture tell us about the way Jesus expressed his feelings?

4. In a nutshell, what does the Bible teach about feelings?

5. How can our feelings help us serve the Lord?

6

Feelings Transformed

Christian teaching on feelings recognizes that emotions often prompt us to act ineffectively or even unrighteously. This is evident in the words of Jesus: "But when the disciples saw him walking on the sea, they were terrified, saying, 'It is a ghost!' And they cried out for fear. But immediately he spoke to them, saying, 'Take heart, it is I; have no fear'" (Mt 14:26-27). And on Tabor, when Jesus was transfigured before Peter, James and John: "And a voice from the cloud said, 'This is my beloved Son, with whom I am well pleased; listen to him.' When the disciples heard this, they fell on their faces, and were filled with awe. But Jesus came and touched them, saying, 'Rise, and have no fear'" (Mt 17:5-7).

We misunderstand if we think that in such

passages Jesus is condemning the feeling of fear. In these and other situations, an event fills the followers of Christ with fear, and they behave in ways that show that fear is dominating them. When Jesus tells them to have no fear, he is not commanding them to suppress their emotional reaction. He is instructing them not to indulge in weak and timid behavior. He might have said, "Do not cry out fearfully!" or "Do not fall down in fear!"

Jesus also taught that while desire is good, it can urge us into serious wrongdoing. "You have heard that it was said, 'You shall not commit adultery.' But I say to you that every one who looks at a woman lustfully has already committed adultery with her in his heart" (Mt 5:27-28). Was the Lord condemning all sexual desire? No, for such a teaching would run counter to the purposes of his Father, which, in fact, Jesus reinforced (Mt 19:4-6). He was speaking against letting sexual desire run wild in our imagination. He was not telling us to stop having sexual feelings, but to stop following them into unrighteousness.

The scriptural approach to feelings involves making sure that our response to their prompting is in line with God's standards of right and wrong.

Reaction and Response

To understand the scriptural teaching it is necessary to understand an important truth about emotions. Every emotion has two components: reaction and response. These elements are always interwoven, sometimes to the point of being indistinguishable. A man is provoked to rage and he slaps his opponent in the face almost simultaneously. The reaction and the response seem to be the same.

An emotional *reaction* refers to the inner movements we experience when a feeling stirs in us. We are familiar with the spectrum of internal states for they are common to all. We flood with delight when a friend returns from a long trip and calls us; we fill with fear when a careening automobile appears about to crash into us. Delight, fear, and all reactions are signals demanding some action on our part. We feel urged to show some affection to our friend who has returned, or we feel motivated to swerve our car out of the path of the oncoming vehicle.

Our *response* is what we do or say under the influence of the reaction. We can act immediately: we become outraged and we slap someone. Or we can respond to a reaction later: we decide to welcome our friend back with a surprise party; we decide to insist that the city install a stop sign at a hazardous intersection. In these latter instances, our response is at first internalized as a decision we make to act in the future.

When Scripture refers to a feeling, it is usually speaking about what we do in response, rather than about how we experience the internal reaction. As we have seen in the passages quoted previously, Jesus seems most interested in the disciples' response to fear and in how a person responds to sexual feelings. When Ezra's grief moved Israel to repent, Scripture described what Ezra did, not how he felt. He wept, rent his garments, fasted, lay prostrate, and assembled the people. This is not to say that the Bible demeans our reaction, but only that Scripture is most concerned about how we relate to the feeling. The scriptural approach to emotions focuses on our behavior more than on our reaction. By paying attention to our responses to feelings, assuring that in each instance we act righteously, we are using our emotions to strengthen our character as Christians.

We must be careful that thinking in this way about feelings—separating our reactions from our responses—does not lead us to believe that our internal experience of emotions is an evil. To say that we must respond righteously to a reaction does not mean that the inner feeling is bad. To the contrary, a sexual desire or a fear or a guilt feeling might be good and appropriate. However, what we do in response to that feeling can either be good and appropriate or inappropriate and bad. The doing, not the feeling, is the reason for the concern.

Feelings Can Change

Distinguishing reaction and response helps us diagnose our difficulties with feelings and points to solutions, if we stand in need of them, as most of us do. Quite commonly we have many deep, intense feelings that function normally. It probably is good news that Scripture gives its blessing to feelings of anger, fear and sexual desire. Once we discover that internal reactions are basically good, we learn that our biggest difficulty lies in the response we make. But what if our responses have been sinful ones?

If your emotions are not supporting you in Christian behavior, you should first of all know that you can get them to change. That may be a surprising piece of news if you have believed popular notions that feelings are givens, impossible to alter. If you persist in believing that feelings are the truth, the very ground of being, you will not even be likely to entertain the thought that emotions can change. It isn't possible to change prime matter, only to accept it and go from there.

To our great advantage, this is not Christian teaching. The Christian position holds that emotions can be transformed by the power of God. Change comes in two ways. In Christ, we are changed from tip to toe, including our emotional reactions. Second, we can alter our responses so that they conform to Christian standards.

To become a Christian means undergoing a process of radical change. By virtue of Christ's death and resurrection, sons and daughters of Adam change their parentage to join a new human race as sons and daughters of God himself. By repentance, commitment to Christ, and baptism in water and the Holy Spirit, they leave behind their old bondage to sin and self-indulgence. They embrace their new freedom as children of God. This transfer from darkness to light is not merely a change of position or location. Each person is transformed deep down in his or her "spiritual genes" into the likeness of Jesus Christ. The change is not static. Through the Holy Spirit and through continuing repentance and faith, the person becomes more like Christ every day.

Our transformation in Christ affects our

emotions as much as our mind and will. Scripture gives us the example of Peter, a man once dominated by feelings, who became rocklike after he received the Holy Spirit. Fear of the Jews drove Peter to deny that he even knew the Lord. His betrayal and subsequent guilt grieved him deeply, and he repented. Humanly speaking, we should expect fearfulness to mark his behavior for the rest of his life. But something changed after Pentecost. Peter became a different man. How could this man, who cringed in fear a few weeks earlier, stand confidently before the very people who had crucified the Lord? Clearly, Peter had undergone a substantial change in his relationship with the Lord. He was now profoundly united to God, and God's power was at work refashioning him in the likeness of his Son. Thus, a man who was accustomed to submit to fears was able to act courageously in doing God's work. Not that the Holy Spirit eliminated fear from Peter's personality, for that is not how he works. Peter continued to experience the feeling of fear, but he was released from bondage to it. The Holy Spirit enabled him to behave courageously when fear stirred in him and gave him the opportunity to be brave or bold.

These biblical truths apply as much to us now as they did to Peter in the days shortly after Pentecost. Because we are in Christ, we are transformed. Our emotions can also change so that they help rather than hinder our Christian life and service.

As Christians, we can get a particular emotional reaction to work for rather than against us by altering our response to it. This is why it is important to distinguish reaction from response. The distinction reveals an opportunity for change. We may be so used to responding to an emotional reaction in a particular way that we may have never thought to respond differently. But the choice is ours. If a feeling moves us in a good direction, we can follow it. But if our inner agitation seems to drive us to wrongful speech or an evil deed, we needn't obey it. We can decide to respond in a more acceptable way, not allowing the feeling that churns inside of us to lead us into sin.

For example, a man who is dominated by unruly anger and whose rage has wreaked havoc among his family and friends can learn to respond differently. He will not have to suppress his anger or bully it, but he will have to learn to express it righteously. He will be glad to find out that there are some unrighteous situations in which he will be able to get angry and show it with force. Practice can teach him how to channel his anger into a determined effort to do something about the situation that triggered it.

Changing our responses may not be an easy task. We may have responded habitually to certain emotions, creating behavior patterns that are hard to break. But wisdom, time, persistence, and the Lord himself are with us to help us accomplish the desired change.

Making too large a distinction between re-action and response in order to prove that change is possible can be potentially mislead-ing. You could conclude that it's right to stop and reflect about how to behave every time a feeling stirs in you. It is true that, while under-going change in a specific area, you may need to pause and deliberate before acting or speak-ing. If fear customarily provokes you to cow-ardice, getting it to lead to courage instead may involve stopping in your tracks and making a conscious decision to be brave. While some element of deliberation may be necessary, the ideal is that emotions should function well *in-stinctively.* The goal is to reach the point where it is no longer necessary, for instance, to stop and think about the right conduct in response to a surge of anger. Eventually, we should be able to get angry and use our anger instinc-tively to do the right thing.

Feelings as Servants

As we have seen, feelings should not be treated as masters nor regarded as enemies. The Christian view holds that our emotions should be our servants. Our society does not have a service class and most of us have no firsthand experience of what it is like to have the support of servants. I am not advocating that we establish a servant class, but simply making a point about how emotions should work for us. A servant is both subordinate and loyal. He places his strength and resources freely under the direction of the person he is serving, and he cooperates interdependently with all the others in the master's service. A good servant has made a heartfelt decision to please the master. The best way to understand how a servant would relate to us is to think of how we want to relate to the Lord as his servants.

Feelings should serve us. They should place all their energies and resources at our disposal. As good subordinates they should follow our directions, working well with other parts of us—our intellect, will, body, and other feelings— to aid us in living effectively. As loyal servants they should not double-cross us by getting us into trouble. They should promote our welfare by supporting good speech and deeds.

Now we can state a summary of the Christian approach, packing the essential elements into one sentence: *The Lord wants to transform us so that our feelings instinctively support us in righteous living.* With this truth in mind, we can turn our attention to a tested way to get our emotions to work as our servants.

For Personal Reflection and Application

Turning to God for Help

A Christian approach to feelings engages the power of the Holy Spirit to help us get them to be more supportive. Our way of tapping into God's power is prayer.

Find a quiet place where you can be alone with God and spend five or ten minutes in prayer.

- Remind yourself that you are in the presence of the God who loves you. He created you and sent his Son to bring you new life.

- In the Lord's presence, think about your experience of feelings. Ask the Holy Spirit to help you pick one feeling you would like to become more supportive in your life.

- Choose a feeling to pray about. Then tell the Lord all about your experience of that feeling—what you like about it, what you find difficult about it, what good it does you, the problems it gives you, everything.

- Ask the Holy Spirit to help you to respond better to that feeling.

For Discussion

1. An emotion can be described in terms of a reaction and a response. Explain the difference between a reaction and a response.

2. Does Scripture seem to focus more on our emotional reactions or responses? Why?

3. What does it mean for us to become transformed in Christ? How does that transformation affect our feelings?

4. How does distinguishing a reaction from a response provide an opportunity for us to change the way we handle a feeling?

5. What does it take to get our feelings to support us like servants?

7

Making the Choice

Treating our emotions as enemies or masters takes energy. Pushing a feeling down or paying homage to it requires work on our part. It shouldn't surprise us, therefore, that it will take effort to get our feelings to become our servants. If our emotions are misdirecting our actions, we must exert energy to get them back on track.

We are now going to consider a biblically based strategy for handling feelings so that they support our Christian lives. It is not a dressed-up version of the willpower approach or stoicism thinly disguised in Christian terms. What sets this strategy apart from those already described and discredited is its complete dependence on God's power.

The feelings-as-enemy and feelings-as-master approaches rely on the self as the source of power for managing emotions. And the self usually botches the job. The action of the Holy Spirit, on the other hand, is the dynamic principle of change that reforms us and our emotional life. Day by day the Holy Spirit refashions us in the image of Jesus Christ, the model of what people are to be like in the new creation. "And we all, with unveiled face, beholding the glory of the Lord, are being changed into his likeness from one degree of glory to another; for this comes from the Lord who is the Spirit" (2 Cor 3:18). Whatever improvement occurs by the application of this strategy, then, comes mainly through the operation of the Holy Spirit.

The strategy for getting your emotions to work as servants has five elements.

Five Steps
to Get Your Emotions to Work for You

1. Do the right and loving thing in every situation.

2. Exercise your Christian authority.

3. Develop strong, committed Christian relationships.

4. Get help for persistent emotional problems.

5. Yield more fully to the Holy Spirit.

If we want our feelings to become supportive, we must pattern our lives on God's standards and expect our emotions to come into
line. Jesus said to Nicodemus, the Pharisee who
came to him by night: "And indeed, everybody
who does wrong hates the light and avoids it,
for fear his actions should be exposed; but the
man who lives by the truth comes out into the
light, so that it may be plainly seen that what he
does is done in God" (Jn 3:20-21).* In this conversation Jesus praised the man who lives by
the truth, literally, the man who *does* the truth.
He used the word "truth" in the Old Testament
sense, in which it is contrasted to unrighteousness or evil. To "do the truth" means to govern
our lives according to the commandments of
God.

By deciding to shape our behavior in accor-
dance with God's ways, everything in us, including our feelings, will work together harmo-
niously in right conduct. The key is to get our
mind to set directions, our will to enforce decisions, and our emotions to support right actions.

To apply the principle, we can ask ourselves
"what is the right and loving thing to do in this
situation?" At least two voices may answer—
our feelings and the truth. Sometimes they will
say the same thing. Anger and the truth may

tell us that we should discipline a child who has been deliberately and repeatedly disobedient. In such cases, when we behave according to the truth, our emotion is already there encouraging right action. Things are working as they should.

But frequently the voices do not agree. In these instances we must follow the objective standard, no matter how we feel. For example, if fear discourages me from telling the Good News to a dying friend even though it is right to speak to him about the Lord, I must overcome my fear.

An Active Approach

Feelings can change when you decide to do the right thing. When the trainman couples a long line of cars to an engine, he knows that the engine will move forward and the whole line will follow. He would never attach a line of cars to a caboose. It wouldn't go anywhere. Living by the truth is like this. When people follow how they feel, they are attempting to get the caboose to move the train; when they do what is right, they move ahead and their feelings follow.

Scripture commands us to take an active approach to conforming our behavior to the pattern of Christian teaching. "Walk by the

Spirit," commands Paul, "and do not gratify the desires of the flesh" (Gal 5:16). Again, Paul exhorts us to "walk as children of light (for the fruit of light is found in all that is good and right and true), and try to learn what is pleasing to the Lord" (Eph 5:8-10).

Doing the loving thing in every situation requires change on our part, and change is not something we relish. We tend to put off having to alter our wrong behavior; we are too comfortable with it. We make ourselves at home with sinful responses by calling them attractive, even virtuous names:

- Touchy, moody people are said to be "sensitive."
- People who always lose their tempers are "in touch with their feelings."
- People so subject to feelings that they are irresponsible are "free spirits."
- Withdrawn people seething with cold anger are called "humble."

Fancy names like these show that our way of thinking about wrong actions in response to feelings differs from the Lord's. The masquerading of bad emotional responses as attractive qualities blocks our improvement because it keeps us from facing the fact that we need to change. If we are serious about getting our emotions to work right, we will learn to speak accurately about our conduct. It makes a lot of sense to admit that something is a "sin," because then we know how to deal with it. We can repent of responding in a sinful way and expect to see a change in our emotional reactions.

The following true stories illustrate the point:

Irritability: Joe always felt irritable and grumpy in the morning and had no desire to speak to anyone in his family for at least an hour after waking. He excused his behavior by saying, "I have a hard time getting up." When he became a Christian he recognized the bad effects of his conduct on his wife and children and decided to relate well with them at breakfast, no matter how he felt. In a relatively short time he noticed two things: first, family life seemed to be going much better, and second, he no longer was irritable in the morning; he actually liked visiting at the breakfast table.

Anger: Mary often felt angry with a close friend who tended to gossip. Thinking that she was showing patience with her companion's weakness, she swallowed the anger, making it harder for her to relate freely. Finally, Mary decided that the loving response was to express her anger by correcting her friend and offering to help her stop gossiping. Her friend was grateful, and Mary learned to use her anger in the right way.

Joy: Tom was asked to play the piano at his sister's wedding reception. On the night of the big event, he was in a very low mood, and celebrating was the last thing he felt like doing. Realizing that it was right to rejoice with his sister, he danced with the bride, listened to stories, and ate at the banquet. By the time he was to perform, his feelings had caught up with his behavior, and he was enjoying himself a little.

Changing how we feel is more a matter of altering our responses than our reactions. When we do the right thing, our inner feelings will come along all right. Sometimes they come docilely, but sometimes they come kicking and screaming.

Repeated efforts to perform the right external responses to a feeling sometimes work their way inside to change our reactions. For example, a lonely person who works hard at reaching out to others may gradually stop feeling lonely. However, sometimes our reactions do not change very much.

Habitual good behavior in response to a feeling, even if it does not change the inner feeling, can take the edge off of a powerful reaction and sometimes may even change how we experience it. For example, people can achieve some serenity about a desire for alcohol or illicit sex. They can become comfortable with honestly admitting their addictions. However, such disorderly desires may continue to perk inside them, and they must be on guard every day, since the desires may surface vigorously at any time, especially during stressful periods.

We may find ourselves in situations in which we aren't sure how to behave because we don't know the Christian teaching. This need not frustrate us if we understand that the Christian way is available to us. God provides his wisdom to us through Scripture, the teaching of our church, and the experience of other Christians who can instruct us. If we want to do the loving thing but aren't sure what it is, we can turn to these sources for help.

From the Heart

Some people object to the idea of living by the truth because it looks to them like bondage. Conforming their lives to external standards seems restrictive. If living the truth means disciplining their inclinations and saying no to themselves, it doesn't sound Christian to them. But they are mistaken. Anyone who wants to be a Christian must decide to live life according to the Christian way, which is found primarily in Scripture. The more a person lives by the truth, the more evident it will become that binding oneself to obeying God's laws leads to freedom.

My brother Bill is a superb classical guitarist. For more than two decades he has trained himself to play the instrument. By constant discipline and submission to external standards, he has become skilled at performing beautiful music. His mastery of the laws of the instrument has made him free to play well. If Bill handed me the guitar and said, "Bert, you play it," I wouldn't even know how to hold it. My clumsy attempt would produce more noise than music. I don't know the first rules about playing guitar, and because I have never submitted myself to them, I am not free to play the instrument. The same holds true for our Christian lives. If we decide to live according to the truth, everything will work together to produce right conduct. Instead of noise, there will be music.

If we find that submitting our lives to the pattern of Christian teaching is repressive instead of liberating, we may be doing it for the wrong reason. We may be attempting to live as Christians out of fear or concern for what others think of us. The unresolved inner conflict is unpleasant, and we may even have to resort to suppressing some of our reactions. If Christian standards are to free us, we must make a decision that goes much deeper than choosing to live by the truth. We must decide from our heart to give our lives completely to Christ and to obey God from now on, no matter what. Jesus himself taught us about this decision:

> The kingdom of heaven is like treasure hidden in a field, which a man found and covered up; then in his joy he goes and sells all that he has and buys that field.
>
> Again, the kingdom of heaven is like a merchant in search of fine pearls, who, on finding one pearl of great value, went and sold all that he had and bought it (Mt 13:44-46).

In both cases the men found something so valuable that they sought after it wholeheartedly. They desired the treasure so much that they cashed in everything they had to obtain it. Note that neither man simply added his find to his possessions. One man sold his belongings to buy a field where the treasure was hidden. The jewel merchant sold every precious stone he owned in order to possess the one he had found.

These parables teach us what it means to decide to obey the Lord from our heart. At the very core of our person, where we make the choices that orient our whole life—in our heart—we must decide simply that we are always going to do what God wants of us. Once we have made this choice, we won't have to consider again whether we are going to follow the Lord. We need only ask what he wants us to do.

If you have never made this decision before, you can make it now. If you made it in the past and let it slip, you can renew it now.

Choosing from the heart to obey God clears up many things for us, among them even serious emotional difficulties. I know a woman who is currently a reliable leader in a Christian group. Fourteen years ago she was full of fear and self-hatred and confused to the point of being suicidal. In the midst of this emotional pain, a friend spoke to her about deciding from the heart to follow the Lord. Ruth responded and made the decision. As her fundamental orientation to life made a 180-degree turn, and as she began to live according to Christian teaching, Ruth's emotions changed too. Fear and self-hatred subsided, and now, many years later, they have been replaced by confidence in God and in herself.

For Personal Reflection and Application

Turning to God for Help

Choosing to love and obey God from our heart is a pivotal decision that affects every aspect of our lives. This choice simplifies many complexities, frees us from bondages and gets us on the right track.

1. Read again the last section of this chapter, entitled "From the Heart." Pay special attention to the words of Jesus quoted from the Gospel of Matthew.

2. Find a quiet place where you can talk personally to God. Set aside five or ten minutes to pray. In your own words, tell the Lord that you love him and want to obey him from your heart.

For Discussion

1. What does it mean to "live by the truth?"

2. How can repenting for wrong behaviors help us with our feelings? Give examples, from your own experience if possible.

3. How does choosing to obey God from the heart affect our emotional life?

8

Taking Charge

If feelings are to become our subordinates, we must learn to govern their activity instead of letting them govern ours. Our feelings should be directed by the fundamental decisions we make in our hearts, not by the magnetism of external influences. Directing our emotions requires a shift in our mentality and behavior. We must stop thinking that our feelings are more powerful than we are. It is time to dispel the false notion that feelings ought to rule over intellect, will and heart. If our emotions have thrown up the barricades and usurped authority over us, we must remove them from the seat of government and restore our own authority. This is the second element of the strategy for getting our feelings to be supportive: take steps to bring order into your emotional life. We must exercise our authority as sons and daughters of God over our emotions.

Five Steps
to Get Your Emotions to Work for You

1. Do the right and loving thing in every situation.
2. **Exercise your Christian authority.**
3. Develop strong, committed Christian relationships.
4. Get help for persistent emotional problems.
5. Yield more fully to the Holy Spirit.

Christians often fail to understand that they have been invested with a substantial degree of authority. As a result, they allow it to lie dormant. When we became Christians we entered into a particular relationship with God. He adopted us as his sons and daughters, conferring upon us all the benefits that belong to his children. Among these are our inheritance, identity, access to the Father, and authority.

Our adoption as sons and daughters marks our incorporation into the new creation, a new humanity re-created out of the race descended from Adam. The relationship that we have with the Father should distinguish us among all human beings, especially in the exercise of Christian authority in our lives. However, people who do not know the Lord often do not see anything different about us, partly because we do not use that authority. Our feelings will work the same as everyone else's if we have not dealt with them authoritatively.

One of my family's favorite children's stories illustrates how sons and daughters of God should exercise their authority. Dooley was a giant, the son of enormous father and mother giants, but he had never grown beyond the size of normal human children. Dooley played with the children of the village, forgetting for most of the time who he was. Now and then he remembered that he was a giant and tried to do giant-type things, such as scare the children with an occasional "fee, fie, foe, fum!" They only laughed and frightened him more than he had frightened them.

One day a Snortsnoot, a hideous monster, came to the village determined to make a luncheon of Trina, a little girl that Dooley was especially fond of. When the monster grabbed Trina and began to stalk away, Dooley stamped on his tail. One lunch being as good as another, the Snortsnoot dropped Trina to chase Dooley. After fleeing about forty feet, Dooley thought, "Wait a minute, I'm a giant, and giants don't run!" He stopped, turned to face the monster, and shouted, "Fee, fie, foe, fum!" The Snortsnoot stopped in his tracks, startled. No one had ever addressed him like that before. But the really surprising thing, both to the monster and to Dooley, was that Dooley grew several feet taller then and there. The monster and the giant repeated this maneuver three times. By the last time, Dooley was a full-grown giant. The Snortsnoot turned on his heels, fled, and was never seen in the village again.

We Christians are very much like Dooley, forgetting who we are and failing to act according to our true nature. But, to our amazement, using our authority as God's children works. We already have within us the power and authority to direct our lives along the paths God marks out for us. We can take charge of this area, rearrange that one, bring order here, give a command there—and expect our directions to be obeyed by our subordinates: our intellect, will, feelings, and even our bodies.

Exercising authority over feelings means getting them to respond to us like good subordinates. Our goal is for them to become strong, healthy, and supportive, taking their directions from us, not vice versa.

A wise teacher, able to bring order into a classroom full of undisciplined children, provides us with a model for applying Christian authority to our feelings. The teacher is confronted with chaos. Lawlessness has generated disorder, clamor, and fighting among the pupils. What does the wise teacher do in a case like this? She does not simply "lay down the law," because to do so would only cause a rebellion. Instead, she enlists the support of the parents and the principal, engaging their authority to back up her own. Then she makes it clear to the children that she has their parents and the principal behind her. Thus, her position is buttressed by the proper authorities. She proceeds to make a few simple rules in order to eliminate what is absolutely intolerable, and then she enforces them. For the rest, she restores order gradually through fairness, kindness, and firm discipline.

She works with the situation, letting her authority be felt until the children accept it, subordinate themselves to her, and obey her. When a child stands up against her, she reminds him that she is acting on his father's authority and that the principal's office is just down the hall. This gives her more clout, making it unnecessary for her to resort to yelling or pleading with the children. In a fairly short amount of time, she has achieved the peace necessary for instruction.

Another helpful illustration of the proper exercise of authority over feelings can be found in a citizen's assertion of his legal rights. Suppose a dozen burly individuals decide to camp out on a hundred-acre wood in order to strip the land for firewood. If the owner of the wood had to rely on his own authority, enforced by his own physical strength, he might not be able to protect his property. However, he can approach the trespassers with the assumption that he is backed by the legal authority of the state. He can tell them to get off the land unless they want the sheriff to remove them forcibly. He can also threaten them with punishment at the hands of the courts. It might take a little time to obtain justice, but the exercise of authority will handle the situation.

Applying these models to our emotional lives is instructive. It will help us to consider how to exercise Christian authority in several different instances.

Desires. Good Christians may be afflicted with unruly desires throughout their lives. Some troublesome desires may lead to nothing worse than eccentricity, but others can lead to wrongdoing or can take someone uncomfortably close to its borders. Curiosity, the desire to know what is not one's business, may prompt a person to read someone else's mail or to search another's belongings. A Christian man may be pestered by homosexual attractions; a Christian woman may be sexually attracted to a man other than her husband. If these desires hit their mark, they could push their subject into sin. Until the love of God reorients a person's desires, it is necessary to deal with them authoritatively.

This is the biblical approach to desires that tempt us: "In your struggle against sin you have not yet resisted to the point of shedding your blood" (Heb 12:4). With persistent wrong sexual desires we may have to settle in for a long haul, regularly applying our authority as sons and daughters of God. "I belong to God," we can remind ourselves and the desire simultaneously, "and you have to obey me. I do not have to obey you, nor am I going to." The same approach applies to other desires whose fruition causes us to sin or takes us to the border of sinful behavior.

Self-esteem. Feeling bad about oneself and feeling guilty are emotional difficulties that destroy self-esteem. The first erodes self-confidence and the second promotes self-condemnation. Christian authority works to control and to cure both problems.

A Christian with low self-esteem must hold himself to the truth of his goodness and his worth, combatting lies authoritatively. Like the wise school teacher he must stand against feelings that say "no one likes you and you deserve it" by establishing the truth and pointing to his Father standing in the background.

Similarly, if a Christian has dealt with guilt by repenting, then guilt feelings that hang around should leave when dismissed by a word of command, like the one given by the man defending his property. If not, it is right to approach these feelings in the manner prescribed for low self-esteem. Of course, if a person fails to repent, there is no reason why guilt feelings should go away.

Fear. "Fight" is an antidote for fear which depends on the exercise of our authority. People afflicted with anxiety, for example, must have faith in God, but also must fight their way out of it. If a man is anxious because he has lost his job and no prospect is in sight, he must formulate a plan of action. As he struggles to move ahead, he may need to deal firmly with worry. His behavior should declare with authority that anxious feelings are not going to paralyze him, for he is God's son and with his Father's aid he can cope with this personal trouble.

Insecurity is a form of fear that manifests itself in behavior like shyness. A shy person could exercise authority by deciding to make friends no matter how hard it feels. Exercising authority over feelings of fear supports our effort to fight through this problem.

Fear sometimes keeps us from Christian service, such as evangelism, speaking up in a Bible study, or volunteering for work we are skilled to do. A word of command can bring authority to bear, making fear give way to courage.

Does this sound like the willpower approach in disguise? Quite the contrary. Exercising our authority as sons and daughters of God does engage the will, but not in the same way that sheer willpower does. Willpower strategies are rooted in fear of feelings identified as enemies. Such strategies try to bully our emotions. In contrast, the Christian strategy is not hostile to emotions. The Christian exercises authority over emotions out of care for them, wanting them to contribute their part to an effective Christian life.

Anyone with a family can identify with the following illustration. Your child spills something at the table, and you react by feeling angry. You exercise your authority over your feelings by channeling your reaction into an expression of patience. "Okay, Mary, you had an accident. We're going to have to keep a towel near the table until you are a little older and can hold your glass." Inside you determine to help your child learn to hold onto her cup more firmly. Sheer willpower would have forcibly pushed the anger down rather than deal with it constructively.

The willpower approach to feelings systematically leaves out the dynamic principle that makes the Christian approach work—the Holy Spirit. Exercising authority over emotions brings our will into service, but God is the agent of change. It is his authority we exercise when we hold ourselves to the truth against low self-esteem, when we resist a perverse desire, or when we command a guilt feeling or a feeling of fearfulness to leave us alone.

The Christian strategy employs the will as an instrument to control our feelings so that they contribute to our Christian behavior. Willpower is engaged in implementing the choices we make in our heart. If we love doing the will of God and make it our intent to obey him always, we can employ our will to help us reach the goal. The Christian approach uses the will as it was intended, not as a weapon to bludgeon our feelings.

Another element in the Christian approach is missing from the willpower approach: the role of Christian relationships. Relationships are a key to learning to deal with our emotions successfully.

For Personal Reflection and Application

Learning How to Use My Authority as a Child of God

By our baptism into Christ we share in his divine life, including his authority. Most of us, however, unwittingly let that Christian authority lie dormant.

We can learn to use our authority as Christians by applying it in little ways. As we gain experience, we can extend it to bigger areas.

For example, we can train ourselves to say no to something we desire by undertaking a limited program of fasting. This can be done in many ways. Here are some suggestions:

1. Pick something that you like, perhaps dessert, or candy snacks, or a favorite TV program, or some other activity or diversion you enjoy.

2. Decide to "give up" that something for a limited period of time. You can eliminate it entirely from your routine or limit it. For example, you can say that "For the next month I will not eat dessert" or "For the next month I will have dessert only on Saturdays."

3. In your prayer time ask the Lord to help

you engage the spiritual power you have as a Christian to support your will in this exercise.

4. During this month, when you feel like indulging yourself and enjoying whatever you have chosen to "give up," exercise your Christian authority to say, "No, I am a Christian and Christians can discipline their desires."

For Discussion

1. What is the basis for saying that Christians have the authority to govern their feelings?

2. What is involved in exercising authority over your feelings?

3. How can a person use authority to deal with unruly desires?

4. How can exercising authority help a person with low self-esteem or guilt feelings?

5. How can exercising authority help a person face feelings of fear?

6. How does exercising authority differ from the willpower approach to feelings?

9

Love One Another

Our incorporation in Christ has many significant consequences for us, not the least of which involves having committed relationships with other Christians. As we grow in learning to love Christian brothers and sisters, our emotional difficulties will improve and our feelings will begin to work in the right way.

This is so because, as we have seen, feelings work best when subordinated to righteous behavior. When we immerse ourselves in a community of Christian friends, our attention moves away from how we feel to how we behave toward others. Emotional health is a natural by-product of genuine Christian love. As taught and modeled by Jesus, love demands that we place ourselves entirely at the disposal of others, no matter how we happen to feel.

What other interpretation can we give to the Lord's teaching the night before his death: he exhorted his disciples to love one another as he loved them. The healing that comes to emotions through good Christian relationships is the third component of our strategy to get our feelings to support us.

Five Steps
to Get Your Emotions to Work for You

1. Do the right and loving thing in every situation.
2. Exercise your Christian authority.
3. **Develop strong, committed Christian relationships.**
4. Get help for persistent emotional problems.
5. Yield more fully to the Holy Spirit.

The converse is also true and helps us appreciate the point. In social environments where relationships have deteriorated, people tend to have emotional problems. Broken families often produce children who are angry and insecure, not to mention separated husbands and wives who struggle with self-condemnation and anxiety. Human beings do not flourish in situations built on radical selfishness. When we encounter negativity and criticalness, let alone envy and hostility, we feel it and react. Before we know it, we are contributing our share of the poison.

So, bad relationships are a major source of our emotional problems. Scripture sums it up: "Do not use your freedom as an opportunity for the flesh, but through love be servants of one another. For the whole law is fulfilled in one word, 'You shall love your neighbor as yourself.' But if you bite and devour one another take heed that you are not consumed by one another" (Gal 5:13-15).

In a group of Christian friends, everyone works hard at learning and using Christian relational skills. They want their love to be a reality. What brings them together is their decision to serve each other. And so they make a commitment to share their lives in some way. These friends speak well of one another, freely expressing their affection. Encouragement rather than criticism typifies their conversation with each other. If members of the group offend each other, they ask to be forgiven and the offended parties grant forgiveness. Their life together is built upon positive and supportive relationships.

The dynamic created by such an environment of Christian friends promotes emotional well-being. When Christians relate openly, their problems with feelings decrease and may even disappear completely. The following accounts describe two men who had fairly serious emotional difficulties until they formed strong relationships with other Christians.

Joe. Joe is a young man from a lower-class family. As a child he was very fearful of people and protected himself by wearing a variety of masks which kept others from getting very close to him. Joe was also intimidated by low self-esteem; he felt unloved and incompetent. Success wasn't a word in his vocabulary, and after two years of college he quit.

At about that time, Joe came into contact with a large interdenominational Christian community. Many people in the community befriended him, making him feel welcome and appreciated. People liked Joe and told him so. They invited him to visit their homes. One of the leaders became a close friend. This man won Joe's confidence, and the young man felt free to talk with him about his life. From all sides, men and women encouraged Joe, helped him learn more about the Christian life, and praised him for his faithfulness and competence—a real novelty for him.

Now, after about ten years with the community, Joe rarely deals with his old insecurities.

For the most part he is free from emotional problems.

Larry. Larry is a man in his mid-thirties from a middle-class background who lives in a small town. His emotional problems were similar to Joe's, although they were compounded by a measure of suppressed anger. In the past, people had difficulty relating to Larry because they couldn't get him to say very much.

It happened that several Christian families had grown close together in Larry's neighborhood. Ten years ago these people from a small town reached out to him in much the same way that the larger community had welcomed Joe. The men and boys included Larry in their recreation and work projects. He was invited to dine, pray and share weekly with one of the families.

The families formed the core of an evangelistic prayer and Bible study group in a local congregation. As Larry got involved in the congregation, they asked him to assume a share of responsibility for the work. Larry is still quiet in his demeanor, but the positive relationships of the group have dissolved his fear and self-hatred, and he has learned how to deal with his anger constructively.

If we are going to live emotionally healthy

lives, we must master the elementary principles of right Christian relationships. We simply must learn to love one another; we must especially learn to relate to each other in ways that promote emotional health.

We are going to discuss seven such principles, none of which is new, since each is grounded in New Testament teaching. Pastors in New Testament times thought these directions essential to Christian living, and they expected every Christian to implement them.

1. *Express affection and give encouragement to one another.* Peter exhorted us to let our "love for each other be real and from the heart" (1 Pt 1:22)*; and Paul taught us to "give encouragement to each other, and keep strengthening one another" (1 Thes 5:11).* Communicating affection and encouragement have become lost arts in our technological age. It is important that we recover these, since expressing affection assures others of our love. A warm handshake, a pat on the back, even a hug when appropriate, can do immense good. We shouldn't be embarrassed to occasionally tell brothers and sisters that we love them.

We should be so constant in encouraging one another that anyone who listened carefully to our conversation would find that we spent more time strengthening others than in any other single kind of speech. We could replace putdowns with positive reinforcements: "Don't give up now, John, you've done so well and you're only a little way from reaching your goal." "You have a beautiful voice, Mary. Your singing last night was very inspiring." Remember, now, no schmaltz, no flattery, just simple, truthful encouragements.

2. A related principle instructs us to *avoid all negativity, criticalness, competitiveness and complaining.* Various Scripture passages teach this, among them "Judge not, that you be not judged" (Mt 7:1) and "Let no evil talk come out of your mouths" (Eph 4:29). Negative speech harms others, even when we are teasing as a way of expressing affection. Criticalness, competitiveness, and complaining normally indicate that we are self-indulgently pursuing our own desires. Such attitudes will only engender bad reactions in others. We should renounce them and let ourselves approach others in a positive, Christian spirit.

3. We should *be open with other Christians concerning our emotional reactions.* Remember the biblical exhortation to "be in the light" (cf. Jn 3:21). Our feelings have an enormous effect on our behavior and relationships. I am not advising the maudlin practice of sharing intimately described feelings, but simply telling others

what has been going on. For example, a man might tell a fellow Christian whom he trusts that he is fighting against a particularly resilient sexual desire. It is especially important to share reactions we are ashamed of or which constitute outright wrongdoing. Such things do not flourish when exposed to the light.

4. A corollary to being in the light tells us to *repent of reactions that cause problems for others.* This principle is based on Jesus' teaching: "If you are bringing your offering to the altar and there remember that your brother *has something against you,* leave your offering there before the altar, go and be reconciled with your brother first" (Mt 5:23).* The list of offenders is long: self-pity, moodiness, cold anger, being withdrawn, shyness, feeling bad about oneself, touchiness, and so on.

We may think that we needn't repent for reactions that we are experiencing internally. After all, who else knows about them? In truth, such reactions rarely have only an internal effect; they vibrate through our relationships with devastating impact. What hurts another person more, a sharp word or a cold shoulder? Our internal emotional states communicate to others just as harmfully as bad speech does. If a person is moody or touchy, everyone gets the message. Not a word may be spoken, but silence or an icy gesture says it all.

Are self-pity, shyness and feeling bad about oneself attitudes to repent of? Most certainly. People who indulge these dispositions behave in ways that affect others negatively. They should repent of the bad behavior and the reaction at its root. People who claim that they are shy by nature or that their attitudes are simply part of their personality are deciding that change is impossible. But those who repent of self-pity or other negative attitudes open themselves up to the Lord so that he can produce a change. Repentance, it should be noted, means admitting the problem or wrongdoing and asking the Lord and any offended person for forgiveness.

Repenting to others for our wrongful internal states is a tricky piece of business, and we need wisdom to do it right. Normally, it is safe to repent to the people closest to us for moodiness or irritability, because it's a sure bet that they have felt it. However, certain of our ill feelings, which others are not even aware of, should not be communicated to them, but dealt with privately and with the Lord. For example, I may envy someone I know only casually, or I may dislike someone else that I hardly know. If I were to repent to these people, thus making them aware of my feelings, I would probably only create more problems for myself and for them.

5. Attempting to control someone by playing on their feelings is a common practice. We should decide to *stop manipulating others by making them feel guilty.* This kind of selfish behavior creates emotional problems for others. We have all been on the giving or receiving end of this maneuver. A daughter informs her mother that she and her husband plan to celebrate Christmas at home this year, rather than traveling miles to spend it with their parents. After a strained silence, the mother responds, "I understand. Don't worry about your father and me. We'll celebrate somehow. We'll just watch TV or something, though it won't seem like Christmas without you." Communication such as this indirectly informs people that they should feel guilty for inconveniencing us. People have enough emotional problems to deal with as it is, and we needn't add to them. No specific Scripture text states this principle exactly, though I doubt that this kind of manipulation is purely a modern tactic. It is covered by exhortations to kindness and by Paul's description of love, which "does not insist on its own way" (1 Cor 13:5).

6. We should *admonish others when we see*

them do something wrong. We should not hold it in and grow bitter over it. Paul says, "Let the word of Christ dwell in you richly,...teach and admonish one another in all wisdom" (Col 3:16). Paul expects those who know what is right to instruct and correct those who fall into sinful behavior. Simple practices such as a word of brotherly or sisterly correction facilitate healthy emotions among Christians by clearing the air of suspicion and resentment.

7. The final principle is that we must learn to control our anger, for anger in its various forms can do great damage, causing emotional problems for others and destroying relationships. When we get angry for the right reason, we should express our anger righteously, not giving it free rein. We must govern it. Resentment and irritability are forms of anger that are typically sources of emotional "static" among us. As such, they are never right. Paul's directions on the matter are clear: "Never have grudges against others, or lose your temper, or raise your voice to anybody, or call each other names, or allow any sort of spitefulness. Be friends with one another, and kind, forgiving each other as readily as God forgave you in Christ" (Eph 4:31-32).*

This is a select list of principles which foster emotionally healthy relationships. It is not exhaustive. Certainly, there are more steps which could be taken to build stronger Christian friendships. But our goal is merely to get a good start on relating in ways that help free people from emotional difficulties.

These principles are not mysterious; they are straightforward New Testament instructions. We may find them difficult to apply, because our own "flesh" and emotional reactions resist good behavior. That makes the principles doubly good, for they become opportunities for us not only to love our brothers and sisters, but also to grow in the life of the Holy Spirit.

For Personal Reflection and Application

Strengthening Your Personal Relationships

Our whole life goes better when we have wholesome personal relationships. Among other things, our emotional life gets healthier and we can face our feelings more effectively.

Christians should take an active approach to building good relationships, since the Lord has made loving one another the essence of Christian living.

Two simple key Christian principles can help improve our relationships: expressing Christian love and seeking forgiveness for offenses.

1. Take some time to think about the state of your relationships with the people closest to you (your family, roommates, people at work or at school, and so on). Ask yourself the following questions:

a. Do I do things for others that show that I love them?

b. Do I express affection to others?

c. Is there something between me and others close to me? If there is, what can I do to repair the relationship?

d. Have I done something to offend another

person? What would it take for me to ask them to forgive me?

2. You can act on your answers to these questions. For example, you can decide to change your behavior regarding one person close to you. Ask yourself what you can do to speak and act in ways that will make them feel loved. Then do it.

Or you could choose to repair a broken relationship with someone by saying you are sorry for something you did or said.

Remember that you are the one initiating the action and that you cannot always expect others to notice a change in you right away.

For Discussion

1. What impact do negative relationships have on our feelings? Give examples, if possible, from your experience.

2. How can positive personal relationships affect our feelings? Give examples, if possible, from your experience.

3. How do expressing affection and giving encouragement improve our emotional well-being?

4. Why should we repent of emotional reactions that touch the lives of others?

10

Feelings and
the Holy Spirit

The Christian view of feelings offers hope to people who experience difficulty relating to their emotions. Emotions are gifts from God, designed to help us live a strong Christian life.

We have discussed what we can do to respond to feelings so that they become our servants. While our effort is essential, too much attention to the part we play can be misleading, because it obscures the real source of emotional improvement. Most changes in our feelings come relatively unnoticed, the consequence of our relationship to Christ rather than the result of deliberate steps we take.

Catching a Christian vision for emotional health, and learning a strategy to implement it, can be counterproductive if we do not proceed wisely. True, the teaching is not so complex that we must be exactingly sure to get everything right. In fact, it is quite simple. Even so, our urgency to get things to change complicates the process, slowing it down and, perhaps, even bringing it to a grinding halt. We can tend to set our own agenda for getting our emotions to change. We want emotional difficulties that have developed over a period of years to disappear in a matter of days or weeks, and so we jump in with both feet to make it happen.

We cannot force our emotions to change according to our timetable. If we really want to succeed we will do better to adopt a calmer, more relaxed approach. Most of us will admit to some minor emotional difficulties. We may have one or two that may be fairly serious, large enough to distress us and attract attention, though not crippling.

Five Steps
to Get Your Emotions to Work for You

1. Do the right and loving thing in every situation.

2. Exercise your Christian authority.

3. Develop strong, committed Christian relationships.

4. Get help for persistent emotional problems.

5. Yield more fully to the Holy Spirit.

For those who have severe emotional problems, it may be necessary to seek help from a professional counselor. This is the fourth plank in the Christian's approach to facing feelings. The advice offered in these pages will be of some help to emotionally troubled persons, but it certainly will not meet all of their needs.

A person can improve his physical health by taking steps such as proper diet, regular exercise, and preventive hygiene. He can take curative steps on his own to correct minor problems, like aspirin for a headache. However, when he experiences serious health problems, he must seek the help of a physician.

The same is true for our emotional well-being. Applying the basic steps outlined here can improve a person's feelings. However, you must approach persistent and serious emotional difficulties just as you would approach serious physical illnesses. You need to consult a professional—a psychologist or a psychiatrist. If you need this kind of counseling and do not know where to turn, ask your pastor or a Christian friend to recommend a reputable and reliable professional.

It is hardly surprising that we should want to be rid of the whole pack of our problems immediately. But, realistically, we should expect that solutions to such difficulties may take time. A dispassionate, honest assessment of ourselves can be very helpful. We should frankly acknowledge problems that we have, earnestly desiring to overcome them. However, it is up to God to set the agenda. Our job is to cooperate with him, allowing him time and room to work the change in us.

Putting pressure on ourselves may actually make matters worse. As we have seen, focusing on feelings multiplies emotional problems. The only effective strategy is one that is directed outward rather than inward. Our focus should be on doing the right and loving thing in every occasion. As we learn to love our Christian brothers and sisters in emotionally healthy ways, our feelings will become more supportive as our relationships grow stronger and clearer. Finally, we must remember that the real source of healing lies outside ourselves—in the Holy Spirit, who is the true source of change.

Yielding More Fully to the Spirit

The Holy Spirit is the divine agent at work in us to transform us. He instructs us in the Lord's ways, opening our minds to the meaning of Scripture. He acts as our advocate, defending us from the accusations of the enemy. He gives us spiritual gifts to equip us for building up the body of Christ. The Holy Spirit in us accomplishes our adoption as children of God. He moves in us with power to make us more like Jesus Christ. It is this latter role to which we want to pay close attention.

The Spirit moves deftly and quietly, and some changes come without our viewing the process. At times he works in us even though we haven't asked for help in a specific area. But we can learn to yield ourselves to him more completely in order to hasten our growth to maturity as Christians. We can present ourselves to him in a way that exposes our weaknesses so that he can target them with laser-like accuracy.

Learning to surrender our emotional reactions to the Holy Spirit is the fifth component of our strategy. I have saved it for last, though it is a theme woven through our discussion, because it is the most important and should be foremost in our minds.

Five Steps
to Get Your Emotions to Work for You

1. Do the right and loving thing in every situation.
2. Exercise your Christian authority.
3. Develop strong, committed Christian relationships.
4. Get help for persistent emotional problems.
5. **Yield more fully to the Holy Spirit.**

You may think that you are the last person to have difficulty with such things as anger or feeling unloved. It isn't that you don't experience such feelings; you simply don't think that they are problems for you. If you are controlled by anger, you may have been praised for being feisty, or if you feel bad about yourself, you may have been called humble.

Before we can ask the Holy Spirit to help us with an emotional problem, we must admit that we have a difficulty. This kind of honesty places us in a position to receive the Lord's help. If we mistake our emotional problems for virtues, we will remain insulated from God's power and from real and lasting change.

Once we take the first step and acknowledge that we have a problem, we must place it under the Lord's authority. This sounds easy enough in principle, but it requires a profound shift in attitude. We must let our problem become God's problem. Too often we tell God that we have a difficulty, perhaps with sexual desire. After we ask for his help, we proceed to handle the desire on our own. Yielding to the Holy Spirit means stepping aside and letting him handle whatever we bring to his attention, or whatever he brings to ours. Of course, such yielding is not license to give in to the desire or to follow it to some unrighteous act.

To place any difficult problem under the Lord's authority, we must direct it to him. For example, to a lustful desire we might say, "I am not going to listen to you; you need to make your plea to the person in charge here and that is the Holy Spirit. Go depict your fantasies to him." That shifts the burden for the cure to the Lord, and leaves us to do the right thing, which is our proper business.

Quite often we fail to experience the full power of the Holy Spirit because we do not really want to change. We are comfortable with our personal set of problems and may even consider them part of our personality. If we do not learn to *hate* those characteristics which make us most unlike Christ, we will hold back the work of the Holy Spirit, who is at work to form us into the Lord's image and likeness. As long as the man with lustful desires enjoys the entertainment they provide, he is not about to change. His heart is not in it. If, in our heart, we love the ways of God, we will find ourselves hating tendencies that are repugnant to him. Once our heart is in it and we begin to want the Holy Spirit to change us, then change becomes possible, but only then.

Finally, if we want the Holy Spirit to change our feelings, we must believe that he has sufficient power to accomplish the change. We can be tempted to settle for less than we should because we simply do not believe that the Holy Spirit can deal with emotional problems as large as ours seem to us. Such an attitude places our difficulty beyond the reach of grace and prevents us from obtaining the only real help available for our cure.

The transformation of our emotions depends upon the exercise of the right kind of faith. We are not speaking here about faith in the existence of God or faith in doctrinal truth, but of expectant faith which enables us to tap into the power of the Holy Spirit. When we place an area under the Lord's authority, we must also believe that he will take care of it. The Lord's power is already released in us—it is there within us waiting for us to engage it.

Consider two analogies. Radio waves exist invisibly all around us. But they go unheard until we switch on the radio dial. Similarly, the internal combustion engine in our automobile generates enormous quantities of energy that would go wasted unless we depress the clutch and direct the power to the drive shaft and wheels. Expectant faith works much like turning the switch on the radio or engaging the clutch in an auto. By it we activate the power of the Holy Spirit, which otherwise would have been wasted, available for our use but allowed to lie dormant.

The Holy Spirit wants to deal with our emotional problems so that our feelings support our Christian lives. The best way for us to cooperate with his initiative is to expect that he can handle any problem no matter how difficult it may seem to us.

The good news about our feelings is that they can help us live a strong Christian life. Contemporary approaches to emotions that view them either as masters or as enemies are based on half-truths which ruin the capacity of our feelings to help us. If we allow our emotions to control us, we defeat the purpose for which they were given. Perhaps they are not yet mobilizing us for effective living. But, by letting the Holy Spirit transform us, we can strengthen our feelings so that they at least do not hinder us and at best they work for us, helping us live effective Christian lives.

For Personal Reflection and Application

Yielding to the Holy Spirit

We need to engage the power of the Holy Spirit if we are going to face our feelings more effectively. The real work of changing us is his, but we can take some steps to make ourselves more receptive to his actions.

Praying about your feelings was introduced in Chapter Six. The following application repeats some approaches suggested there and adds some ways to yield our feelings to the Holy Spirit:

• Remind yourself that you are in the presence of the God who loves you. He created you and sent his Son to bring you new life.

• In the Lord's presence, think about your experience of feelings. Ask the Holy Spirit to help you pick one feeling you would like to become more supportive in your life.

• Choose a feeling to pray about. Then tell the Lord all about your experience of that feeling—what you like about it, what you find difficult about it, what good it does you, the problems it gives you—everything.

• Ask the Holy Spirit to help you respond better to that feeling.

• You must want to experience a change in the area. Be honest with yourself and with God. If you are not ready to change, tell God you are not yet ready to change. You can ask him to help you be willing to change.

• Ask the Lord to help you with the feeling and expect him to act. When the feeling affects you, you can direct it to the Lord. For example, you can tell an unruly desire to speak to the Holy Spirit instead of to you, which shifts the burden from you to him.

• This Christian approach works to help us face our emotions every day. However, people with persistent and deep-seated emotional or psychological problems should pray for the Spirit's help, but they must also seek professional help, which is another way the Lord uses to help us face our feelings.

For Discussion

1. Why should we avoid working too hard to change the way we respond to our feelings?

2. What steps can we take to yield an emotional problem to the Holy Spirit?

3. What is "expectant faith?" How does it help us receive God's power in our lives?

Notes

1. William Treadwell, quoted in "How to Motivate Yourself and Others," *Leadership* (Summer Quarter 1980), p. 15.

2. Fr. Frank Burke, "The Art and Advantage of Journaling," *Marriage Encounter* (February 1981), p. 8.

3. On the impact of technological society on the emotions, see Stephen B. Clark, *Man and Woman in Christ* (Ann Arbor, Michigan: Servant Books, 1980), p. 18.

4. See Paul Vitz, *Psychology as Religion* (Grand Rapids, Michigan: Eerdmans, 1977), chapter 1.

5. Theodore Isaac Rubin, *Compassion and Self-Hate* (New York: Balantine, 1975), p. 218.

6. David Viscott, *Language of Feelings* (New York: Pocket Books, 1977), p. 22.

7. Rubin, pp. 218-219.

8. Rubin, p. 219.

9. "Dialogue on Feelings," *The New Spirit* (newsletter of Marriage Encounter in Queensland, Australia) (February 1979), p. 2.

10. Hal Edwards, "Religion Plus Psychology Equals What?" *The Candle* (October 1979), p. 1.

11. Bruce Larsen, *The Relational Revolution*, p. 58.

12. Kevin Perrotta, "Feelings As Guide, Goal, and Ground of Being," *Pastoral Renewal* (November 1979), p. 37.

═══ St. Paul Book & Media Centers ═══

ALASKA
750 West 5th Ave., Anchorage, AK 99501   907-272-8183

CALIFORNIA
3908 Sepulveda Blvd., Culver City, CA 90230   310-397-8676
5945 Balboa Ave., San Diego, CA 92111   619-565-9181
46 Geary Street, San Francisco, CA 94108   415-781-5180

FLORIDA
145 S.W. 107th Ave., Miami, FL 33174   305-559-6715

HAWAII
1143 Bishop Street, Honolulu, HI 96813   808-521-2731

ILLINOIS
172 North Michigan Ave., Chicago, IL 60601   312-346-4228

LOUISIANA
4403 Veterans Memorial Blvd., Metairie, LA 70006   504-887-7631

MASSACHUSETTS
50 St. Paul's Ave., Jamaica Plain, Boston, MA 02130   617-522-8911
Rte. 1, 885 Providence Hwy., Dedham, MA 02026   617-326-5385

MISSOURI
9804 Watson Rd., St. Louis, MO 63126   314-965-3512

NEW JERSEY
561 U.S. Route 1, Wick Plaza, Edison, NJ 08817   908-572-1200

NEW YORK
150 East 52nd Street, New York, NY 10022   212-754-1110
78 Fort Place, Staten Island, NY 10301   718-447-5071

OHIO
2105 Ontario Street (at Prospect Ave.), Cleveland, OH 44115   216-621-9427

PENNSYLVANIA
510 Holstein Street, Bridgeport, PA 19405; 215-277-7728

SOUTH CAROLINA
243 King Street, Charleston, SC 29401   803-577-0175

TENNESSEE
4811 Poplar Ave., Memphis, TN 38117   901-761-2987

TEXAS
114 Main Plaza, San Antonio, TX 78205   210-224-8101

VIRGINIA
1025 King Street, Alexandria, VA 22314   703-549-3806

CANADA
3022 Dufferin Street, Toronto, Ontario, Canada M6B 3T5   416-781-9131